That's Fourpence You're Eating!

Flashbacks

The Flashback series is sponsored by the European Ethnological Research Centre, c/o the National Museums of Scotland, Chambers Street, Edinburgh EH1 1JF
General Editor: Alexander Fenton

Other titles in the Flashback series include

That's Fourpence You're Eating!

A Childhood in Perth

Frances Rimington

Birlinn

IN ASSOCIATION WITH
THE EUROPEAN ETHNOLOGICAL RESEARCH CENTRE
THE NATIONAL MUSEUMS OF SCOTLAND

First Published in 2006 by
Birlinn Limited
West Newington House
10 Newington Road
Edinburgh
EH9 1QS

www.birlinn.co.uk

ISBN10: 1 84158 407 X
ISBN13: 978 1 84158 407 2

British Library Cataloguing-in-Publication Data
A catalogue record for this book is available from the British Library

The publisher acknowledges subsidy from the Scotland Inheritance Fund
towards the publication of this book

Designed and Typeset by Wordsense Ltd, Edinburgh
Printed and bound by Antony Rowe, Chippenham

Contents

Illustrations

11. d) Bassinette iron frame, string sides, trimmed with
       drapery
    e) Perambulator
    f) Baby's bottle
    g) Mail-cart
    h) My 'home-made' bicycle
    i) Cat-toys
12. a) Glengarry bonnet
    b) Sausage curls
    c) French knot
    d) Empire style evening dress for 'coming-out' ball
    e) Cousins Jane and Fanny Espinasse with hearing aid
13. Frances Rimington as a flapper *c.* 1905
14. Diana Brisco Malik (née Rimington)
15. John Hill Thomas, Captain 4th V.B. Blackwatch R.H.,
    1900–1907 (6.9.1862–12.1939)

Foreword

HAVING recently finished my notes on the House of Gordon, and the dark days of winter being upon us, I find myself at a loss for occupation – so I now start on a little 'history' of myself and what it was like living in the Victorian '90s and the time of Edward VII, with part of the reign of George V, for your interest and, I hope, entertainment.

Although life was much more conventional and formal in my early days, I am glad I lived then. Apart from the South African War, conditions generally were peaceful and more carefree – at least it was for people like ourselves.

No doubt this is a selfish way of looking at things, because for many life was much harder – yet on the whole people are less content in all ranks of life nowadays.

So the picture I have drawn of life is only one side of it – one lived in one's own immediate circle, and except for a few privileged people there was little going from place to place. Holidays abroad were only for the well-to-do, and apart from the annual holiday in the country or at the sea one stayed put in the place where one was born.

I hope you will enjoy reading this book as much as I have enjoyed writing it.

Frances Rimington

Note

Mother left these memoirs in various states of completion, sometimes under headings, sometimes not, partly typed, partly rewritten, but mostly as notes and jottings in a variety of notebooks and exercise books and on all shapes and sizes of paper, back and front and up along the margins. I have tried to gather them together under the headings she had drawn up and also adhere to her chronological approach and retain her style. Some parts may seem inconsequential and verbose, but, except to avoid repetition, the temptation to cut and condense was resisted so that the essential spirit of the times and her memories of them was not lost.

The illustrations are traced from her notebooks.

Jean Gordon Cobbald

Part One:
Frances Emily Hill
Rimington, 1890–1973
(née Thomas)

Introduction:

My Birth, My Parents and My Grandparents

Leerie, leerie, licht the lamps,
Lang legs and crookit shanks.

FOUR years old. My earliest memories date back to when I was this age, and one of them is watching the lamplighter at dusk on his rounds with his torch flaring at the end of a long pole and the gentle flame of the gas lamps springing into life at his touch. Another memory is of a poor mangy brown bear led by a gypsy type of man; a short pole was fixed to a ring in the bear's nose by which the man led him round and he ambled in a clumsy dance while his master churned out some wheezy tunes from a small organ which was suspended from his shoulders by a strap and supported from below with a single leg.

At other times a tiny pathetic monkey was brought dressed in little blue breeches and a red military coat.

He sat on top of the organ attached to it by a light rope and he would get up and dance when urged to do so by the man.

I was taken out to give biscuits and pennies to these poor animals in return for their entertainment, feeling rather afraid of the bear it must be confessed. I much preferred to give the pennies into the hand of the tiny monkey.

We also had visits from 'pifferari' men – real vagabonds in appearance, wearing loose, rusty garments with rough undressed leather boots and their trousers cross-gartered with narrow strips of leather. They wore coats of sheepskin and slouch felt hats with a long feather stuck in the band. A large drum hung from their backs and was beaten with sticks tied to their elbows; on the top of the drum a pair of cymbals were fixed and these were worked by a cord fastened to the man's heel so that when he moved his leg up and down the top cymbal was raised and fell with a clang on the lower one. As the man marched along he played gay tunes on a long thin pipe.

> To whom related and by whom begot.
>
> (Pope)

When I was born on December 20th, 1890 at 6.40 a.m. my parents were 28 and 25 and were living at 8 Rosemount Place in Perth. I was christened in the house by Dr Anderson, the clergyman of the parish of Kinnoull (who had officiated at the marriage of

Effie Gray of Bowerswell to John Ruskin in 1848; she was later married to Millais). At this period weddings, christenings and funerals were frequently held in the houses; it was not obligatory for them to be held in church. The Crown Derby punch bowl I have served as a font and was lent by my grandfather Thomas.

My father was a solicitor and became a partner in the firm of Thomas and MacLeish of which my grandfather was senior partner. At the time of my father's retiral in 1923 this firm became amalgamated with that of Condie, Mackenzie and Co., some of whose partners were appointed as my trustees.

My grandfather Thomas was Sheriff Clerk of Perthshire, an office he held for over fifty years, and was a light in the legal world of Perth. In Scots Law the Sheriff Principal is the Chief Magistrate and Judge of the county, whilst in England his duties are ministerial rather than judicial. The Sheriff Clerk in Scotland is the Registrar of the Sheriff's Court and has charge of all the records. My grandfather Thomas came of well-to-do farming people near Alyth, where they owned a large farm called the Cotton of Craig. This name must be derived from the old district called 'cot-toun' where cotters lived, in the same way as 'Kirktoun' where the church was and 'Milltoun' where the mill was were.

Grandfather Cornillon [Hypolite William] was French and his father came to Edinburgh at the time of the French Revolution. He was born in Edinburgh and was educated at the Edinburgh Academy. Among my books you will find a prize he won, not unnaturally, for French recitation. Great-grandfather Cornillon [Hypolite Joseph Emil Germain] had worked as a teacher in Edinburgh and married Helen Neaves, who was sister to Lord Neaves, a Scottish judge. There were many legal connections in my family.

My mother's father was also in legal business in Edinburgh and was a Writer to the Signet, which is an ancient society of solicitors in Scotland who had the Supreme Court of Justice, and still have the exclusive privilege of preparing crown writs, which include all charters, precepts and writs from the Sovereign or Prince of Scotland.

Father and Mother met when he was serving his apprenticeship in grandfather Cornillon's office in Edinburgh. Later my father's younger brother Arthur Thomas also served his apprenticeship there and later became a partner in the firm Cornillon, Craig and Thomas which exists today most probably under other partners' names. Arthur married my mother's youngest sister, Ethel Cornillon. My mother and father were married on 10th February, 1890 in St Giles Cathedral, Edinburgh.

Figure 1: The Thomas Family

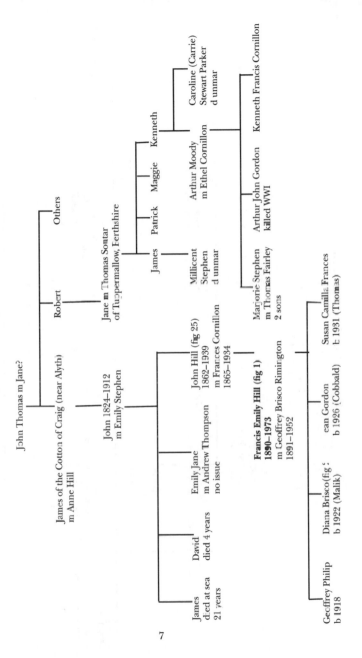

Figure 2: The Cornillon Family

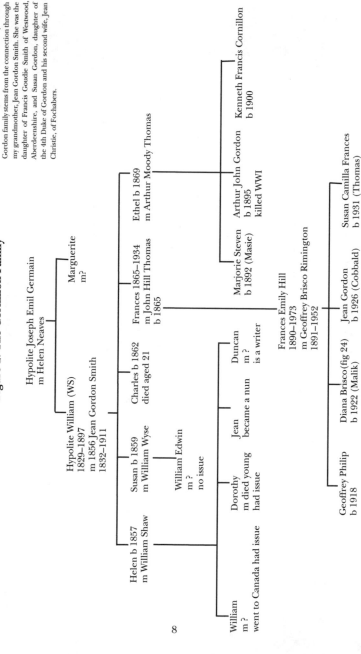

Note: A lifelong interest in the history of the Gordon family stems from the connection through my grandmother, Jean Gordon Smith. She was the daughter of Francis Goudie Smith of Westwood, Aberdeenshire, and Susan Gordon, daughter of the 4th Duke of Gordon and his second wife, Jean Christie, of Fochabers.

8

1

Homes

The world has nothing to bestow;
From our own selves our joys must flow,
And that dear hut – our home.
                              (N. Cotton)

COMELY BANK, PERTH

WHEN my parents married they had an income of approximately £500 a year. They first lived in a tiny house in the Comely Bank area not far from the house which was their last one. When my arrival was expected they moved to 8 Rosemount Place, quite near to their first house. Here they lived until 1899 when we moved to a semi-detached house, Northfield, overlooking the North Inch in Perth, one of the farthest-out houses to be built in that district at the time. But it was not long until buildings sprang up all around, and the fields which had surrounded us

9

vanished and the uninterrupted view to the northern hills was hidden.

In 1912 another move took place, back again across the river to Gaskhill which stood high overlooking the river and town. We were there for only a short while before moving to St Albans a little further along the Dundee Road – as far as I remember about 1915; this was the last house in which I lived at home with my parents. I visited them there with Philip and Diana [Frances Rimington's children] as babies. Then they left Perth for a time in about 1923 to live at Blairgowrie, returning to Perth in 1927 or 1928 to 4 Comely Bank, where we all spent several holidays with them.

Mother died in 1934 and Father in 1939, so mercifully they had no experiences of World War Two conditions.

8 ROSEMOUNT PLACE, PERTH

I have quite a clear memory of 8 Rosemount Place, and so have drawn a small plan of it, but not accurate to scale [see plate section]. All the houses of this period were very dark in appearance, decorated in sombre colours with most of the woodwork of mahogany or dark-stained deal. Only in the drawing-rooms and bedrooms was there any lighter paint but even then it was usually grey or soft blue with a dull surface – never gloss white. In houses where there were portraits in gold frames the walls were coloured a plain dull green to show them off. All the furnishings were of sage-green, red or brown serge edged with wool gimp from which bobbles hung at intervals.

Our dining-room was papered in dark browny-green with large gilded floral pattern, with dark paint, dark oak suite of large expanding table with solid carved legs, a sideboard with mirrors, six chairs upholstered in brown leather, a 'what-not', which was a set of tall shelves tapering to the top, and a Davenport – a sort of writing desk. The pictures were etchings of Raeburn portraits and of landscapes by well-known artists, all in monochrome with no colour anywhere.

Upholstery on sofas and armchairs was of plush or horsehair, woven into a kind of cloth and exceedingly harsh on the backs of little bare legs. Windows were always draped with lace curtains as well as serge ones and these hung from massive brass or wooden curtain poles ending in a large knob. The rings were about 3 inches in diameter. This type of pole has come into fashion again recently. All very heavy and stodgy.

There were always blinds to draw down at night; in the main rooms there were wooden Venetian ones and in the other rooms they were of glazed linen in natural colour or dark green, sometimes both. One could draw either or both. Bedrooms had chintz curtains in floral designs. The wallpapers in the bedrooms and drawing-rooms were also colourless in nondescript greys and washy blues.

The general effect was somewhat depressing as well I remember, especially at night as all the lighting in houses until about 1900 was from the simple 'fish-tail' gas jets, which gave very poor light. There was usually a chandelier in the centre of large rooms with three burners and coloured globes but hardly ever were more than two of these lit at once for the sake of economy. In the bedrooms there was only a single light with a plain globe, either fixed on the wall or on the mantleshelf. In medium-sized public rooms there might be two wall lights. There were no bedside lights, only a candle to save getting into bed in the dark after putting out the gaslight. No reading in bed – bad for the eyes. When we moved to Northfield, we had incandescent gas burners which gave a much better light even though the fitments were much the same – wall brackets and a central three-burner chandelier.

The drawing-room was upstairs as was the fashion at this time, and had a bluish-grey paper and more dark curtains. The fireplace was also draped to match with plush – highly dangerous, one would think – and had a mirrored overmantel with little shelves where many china ornaments were displayed and needed much dusting. Firescreens, like embroidered banners and hung from an adjustable bracket clamped with a thumbscrew to the mantelshelf, were in common use and were intended to preserve the ladies' complexions from the heat of the fire.

Palmleaf fans as decoration were fashionable along with peacocks' feathers and bullrushes arranged in a length of bamboo which hung in the corner of the room. Many of the pictures were chrystoleums or oleographs painted by my mother. These were photographs of well-known paintings treated with oil until they were transparent then pressed down against convex glass and painted at the back with oilpaints, well mixed with Chinese white. The picture was framed with a 3-inch-wide plush frame – grand dust collectors, but they were thought very pretty and artistic.

A chiffonier (cabinet) was always a feature of drawing-room furnishings, with a mirrored top to match the overmantel. On this were displayed glass, china and silver objects. Little occasional tables and spindly occasional chairs, a sofa or ornamental settee, and an upright piano completed the 'best' room which was used on state occasions only. If there was no third public room such as a parlour, the dining-room was always in daily use by the adults, small children being confined to their nurseries. All tabletops were covered with green serge or plush and trimmed with gimp braid with chenille bobbles. There was a matching curtain over the door.

The room downstairs behind the dining-room was my nursery. It faced north-west and so the only sunshine that ever reached it was at about 5 p.m. in the summer. My nurse and I slept there and had our meals there. My cot, her bed, a washstand, a small cupboard for our cutlery and condiments etc, a table and a wicker chair for Nurse and my little chair for me, lino on the floor with a rug in front of the fire and the usual large nursery fireguard were the furnishings. I think there was a screen behind which Nurse no doubt discreetly performed her ablutions and dressed. This room must have had very little floor space, as the house was not a large one, and been nice and fuggy into the bargain.

I remember a cow covered in real hide stood on the mantelpiece, and when its head was pushed to one side, it moved. The legs were fastened to a green board with wheels and it could be pulled along. I possessed a stuffed rag cat and two kittens – just an outline shape with details painted on. A dearly loved toy was a white rabbit-fur monkey with a long tail and two rows of little white beads stitched on his face for teeth, and I never loved him better than when all his fluff was worn off and he was shiny leather and his teeth hung down like a double-row pearl necklace.

My parents' bedroom was over the nursery, with wallpaper of a grey tone and the paintwork dull grey to match. There was a brass bedstead, a heavy dark mahogany suite and a washstand. All beds in the house were iron-framed, black japanned or brass with knobs at each corner; no spring mattresses, only thin iron slats crossing the framework. Then came two straw-filled palliasses and a horsehair mattress on top of them. Every bedroom had its marble-topped washstand with 'set' – jug, basin, soapdish, toothbrush jar, a water carafe and glass. Hot water for washing was brought in a can to the bedroom by the maid and placed in the basin covered by a towel or blanket cosy. The cans were enamelled light tan with scarlet or blue touches, but in grand households they would be brass requiring weekly cleaning and polishing. Certain houses without bathrooms as yet had 'sitz-baths' in the bedrooms in which you sat but your legs hung overboard. The men washed and shaved in the bathroom but hot water was brought to the bedrooms again to wash before going to bed. Beds were turned down and bottles (stone) were put in. All this went out with World War One.

The staircase and hall had a very dark green and brown paper and deal woodwork. The hall light had a bunsen burner which unless one was going up or down stairs was kept at a bunsen 'peep'.

The maid's room was a tiny one over the front door just the width of the hall with space for only one. When later I had no nurse, we had a second maid, a young girl of sixteen who combined the duties of house-tablemaid with that of nursemaid to me. We then slept in a bedroom over the kitchen, and the nursery was used as a daily sitting-room by us.

This bedroom and the bathroom were up a flight of three or four steps in the back part of the house. The bathroom was panelled all in deal boards. The basin, bath and 'seat' were all boxed in with deal panelling; the bath was painted as marble of yellowish ground and red and green squiggles; the basins of the lavatory and washbasin were in blue willow pattern design. The lavatory flushed by a handle which one pulled up from a depression at one's right hand.

The kitchen walls were painted grey and of course all the cooking and water heating was done by a range. This meant a lot of work as the flues had to be cleaned out once a week at least and the front blackleaded, and the trimmings of steel, the fender and the fire-irons had to be burnished with emery paper, or a cloth and wet ashes – a dirty and tedious business. The table and dresser were of plain white wood which had to be scoured weekly. There were a couple of plain wood chairs and a wicker chair for when the maid had time to take her ease. Off the kitchen, there was a larder, pantry and a wash-house with a boiler in one corner and a fitted washtub with hot and cold taps. Once a week an old body called Mrs Burgoyne came to wash everything barring table linen and my father's stiff collars and shirts which went to the laundry. She had her breakfast and dinner and 2s 6d in her pocket; after hanging out the washing she departed and the rest of the drying, mangling and ironing was attended to by the two maids.

On the kitchen wall was a row of bells graduated in size so that their sound indicated from which room they were being rung. These were worked by wires running from each room – one pulled on a lever or pulled on a long thick rope. In large establishments there would be an indicator board in the butler's pantry with little discs that waggled over the name of each room. In some houses a bell rang from the master bedroom to the maid's room, so if Madam did not hear Mary Jane bestirring herself in the morning she was roused by the bell.

Under the row of bells in the kitchen hung a graded row of six silver-plated or pewter dish covers – more weekly cleaning. All firegrates of course required blackleading daily when the fire was cleaned out in the morning. The maids had the kitchen fire and at least one public room fire to see to, the dining-room to sweep and dust, ditto the staircase and hall and breakfast to get ready after these chores. The master's shoes had to be cleaned ready so it was necessary to be up betimes, especially if he wanted hot water for shaving or bath. Range-heated hot water did not arrive quickly; the water was often not very hot unless the flues were kept very clean and the proper dampers pulled out to direct the heat towards the water-heating part of the range. One could not cook on top or bake in the oven and have hot water all at once.

At the outbreak of World War One, I tried my hand at cooking on a range when for the first time we were without maids, and jolly difficult it was too. The wretched things consumed vast quantities of coal but when I was a small child it was only 14s 6d a ton and therefore not so costly. On washing days a separate fire was lit under the boiler copper for boiling the whites. Occasionally a very primitive and clumsy gas cooker was used but not in our house – it was considered extravagant to have two means for heating water and cooking.

All the saucepans were iron and very heavy. Knives were cleaned on a board covered with a piece of leather. A cork was dipped in some dark brown 'Knife powder' and rubbed up and down on the knife blade until the stains disappeared – stainless steel cutlery was not known. Scouring powder was in a cake about the size of a piece of soap; this was the famous 'Monkey Brand' which disappeared when powdered varieties came onto the market in the 1900s.

After World War One the staff was reduced to one and after the second to none. Madam now does it herself very efficiently, with a job as well, thanks to modern gadgets.

There was a tiny flower garden in the front of the house and a washing green at the back where I played in the summer. Mother liked gardening but made no attempt to grow fruit or vegetables.

When I was little there were no motor cars (they came in 1905–06), no radio, few telephones except for business people, doctors and the like. They were a luxury not enjoyed by ordinary people. The apparatus consisted of a tiny box hung on the wall; you first obtained the exchange by turning a handle, then gave the operator the number you required. The good thing about them was that if someone rang you and you did not get to the phone in time, the operator would tell you who had phoned.

NORTHFIELD, PERTH

When I was eight we moved from Rosemount Place to a newly built semi-detached house called Northfield overlooking the North Inch, one of the last in a row. There was a very pleasant outlook from our front windows as we could watch folks going round the golf course.

Until I was about ten, I was not allowed to go out alone – a nurse-housemaid would accompany me. Between ten and seventeen I would be sent off in an old growler cab – often journeys of several miles. If the cabman had wished, anything might have happened to me but apparently I was considered safe.

I escaped all the infantile disorders – measles, whooping cough – but was subject to bronchial colds and tummy troubles. Our Doctor Ferguson was a real Victorian type, came in a brougham, was short-bearded and breathed heavily as he listened in to my chest with an early stethoscope. I remember the nauseating Gregory powders he prescribed for my tummy troubles, administered in a spoonful of jam which ill-disguised its revolting taste. The arrowroot pudding made without milk was exactly like wallpaper paste and was supposed to stay the flux. Fortunately we were all a healthy family so the doctor's services were not much required in an age when health was none too good. So the plain fare I was brought up on speaks well for itself.

We lived at Northfield until 1912 or 1913, when we moved back across to the other side of the river to

Gaskhill, which was the largest house we had occupied so far – standing high and overlooking the town – and this is where I lived until I was married during World War One. I visited the folk at St Albans, another large house but I cannot remember much about it.

25 BAROSSA PLACE, PERTH

Grandpapa Thomas' house, 25 Barossa Place, Perth, was a large self-contained double fronted house. To describe it more easily I have drawn a rough plan [see plates section]. There was a small formal garden in front with a large rockery down one side, where Aunt Millie, who was a keen gardener, grew among other plants a lot of auriculas, the real old Dusty Miller type covered with powdery whiteness. I have often wondered if my love for them stemmed from seeing them here. At the back there was a vegetable garden at one side and a tennis lawn, and round the high walls were apple and plum trees trained against the walls. Croquet was played and I was instructed in the game by my aunts at an early age.

I never saw my paternal grandmother, Emily (née Stephen) Thomas, as she had died when my father was only nine. The old nurse, Margaret McKillop, who brought up my father, was still alive until I was twelve. I can picture her sitting in an armchair by the kitchen fire at 25 Barossa Place in a neat black dress with large white apron and round her shoulders a small black or grey knitted shawl. She wore a white lace cap with a black bow. As was the custom, the old, faithful nurse was given a comfortable home in which to end her days. She had ruled the nursery with a rod of iron and was quick in the use of the 'taws' [leather strap] in cases of misdemeanour. After the children were old enough, she became housekeeper until the daughters were able to take on the household management.

I used to pay a weekly morning visit to these aunts – Emily, Millicent and Caroline – and a little friend Edith (Tootee) Leslie was asked to play with me. A huge wax doll the size of a two year old was brought out to entertain us; its clothes were in the fashion of the 1880s, all handmade, and the doll's hair was real, which I thought very wonderful, but it had the most inane expression on its wax face and the body and upper limbs were of calico, sawdust-stuffed. My Aunt Caroline travelled quite extensively and brought home interesting things from India, Ceylon and other places; one of these was 'jumping beans' which when they were put on a plate by the fire began to jump due to an insect inside. We would be given a cake and milk elevenses and taken to see Pussy's latest batch of kittens in the laundry.

In the summer we played croquet and in the winter the bagatelle board came out. I always enjoyed it when Cousin Lily Bell came to stay with my aunts, her cousins. She was a very amusing lady and had entertaining tales of the people with whom she lived when she went as a governess to France and Spain and Russia.

Of the French Papa who used to exclaim frequently 'Saperlipopette' (A mild French oath derived from *sapristi*) or as he said it, 'Sapairlipaw-pette!' One day she came into the family sitting-room to find the girls unpicking a dress and there was a strong smell, so Cousin Lily asked, 'Qu'est ce que cet odeur horrible?' 'Oh, c'est rien, c'est la robe de Maman!' In Spain and Russia she came in for some stirring revolutionary conditions but survived without any harm – quite an adventure for a woman in 1896. My aunts were rather disconcerted because they foolishly asked me if I liked coming to see them and my reply was 'I like you and Aunt Carrie very much, but THIS is the favourite', pointing to Cousin Lily.

Grandfather was visited on Saturdays and Sundays. He was a short stockily built man with white side-whiskers; he was very healthy and strong and went to business until a month before his death and had all his own teeth when he died aged eighty-eight. He used to entertain me with imitations of an owl, showing how the bird could turn its head so far round – Grandpa rather to my alarm apparently had this same facility. He was generous with little presents of money from time to time and later gave me two or three books for my libraries every three months which started my love of reading and libraries. He was a great cricket enthusiast and attended all the matches on the North Inch ground. He was a tremendous letter writer and kept in touch with friends and relatives all over the world, sending off great bundles of magazines to them. His sister, my great-aunt Jane Thomas, married one Thomas Souter, a farmer; they lived at Tippermallo, near Methven, and I remember spending holidays there and enjoying the huge fruit garden and country farmhouse, but the bed had a wooden slatted base with no springs.

Aunts Millie and Carrie and Grandpa used the parlour as their sitting-room; Aunt Emily, known as The Miss, occupied the drawing-room upstairs in solitary glory until she married very late to everyone's surprise about 1900. I never had more contact with her, just seeing her going in and out dressed rather elaborately with very floral hats tipped forward and always a very thick white veil. She had a bad complexion, for which nothing was done in those days, and no lady ever wore make-up – only actresses and fast women – so she concealed her blemishes, at least when she was out of doors, with the veil. After her departure to her own home, the two younger aunts used the drawing-room. This house had the same dark appearance with solid Victorian furniture but they had electricity installed in 1900.

My Aunt Millie died in 1910 from the effects of an insect bite when on holiday in Aix-les-Bains. Grandpa died two years later and then the house was sold and Aunt Carrie moved about for a time in Perth, Edinburgh and its outskirts and Blairgowrie until her death in 1941 or 1942. My father's eldest brother James went to sea and was lost at sea when twenty-one.

David died aged four. Arthur, the youngest, married my mother's youngest sister Ethel and worked in my maternal grandfather's office in Edinburgh.

The little child's chair which I have was made from the mahogany wood from a four-poster bed which belonged to my great-grandmother; this bed had been given to Margaret McKillop [Nurse] who had the top end cut to a half-tester and had the chair made from the pieces left over for me. I was always a bit of a favourite with her as being 'Maister John's bairn', he being the favourite of the family she had cared for and brought up. She gave me my first gold watch which hung on a fob and which I was only allowed to wear on state occasions.

While Margaret McK was Nurse, the housekeeper after Grandmother's death was a Miss Brodie who, my father used to tell me, was a formidable lady who ruled the roost and everyone in it.

1 DUNDONALD STREET, EDINBURGH

The home of my maternal grandparents was at 1 Dundonald Street, Edinburgh. This was a flat with a doundle [sub-basement] sunk below: the kitchen, larders and servants' bedrooms one stair down and the laundries and store place one below that and letting out onto a tiny drying garden at the back. Adjacent to the house and leading to the house and to the two flats above was what was called 'a common stair', some stone steps with an iron rail. In fact Grandfather's flat was built round this stair as you can see from the plan [see plates section], and one could hear people clattering up and down the stairs. As a child I used to think it was not quite nice that my grandparents had this common stair attached to their dwelling, interpreting the 'common' in the sense of vulgar.

Grandfather was a genial old gentleman; he used to amuse me with his repeater watch which struck the hours; when a knob was pressed I could 'blow' it open, while Grandpapa cunningly pressed a spring – it being a 'whole hunter' watch.

Grannie was a very dignified lady who while being fond of her grandchildren did not come down to their level to amuse them. We were usually given a pile of early volumes of *Punch* and sat up to a table to keep us quiet, which to do us justice, they did. We were very well behaved, I feel.

Grannie used the dining-room as her sitting-room, where she did her mending and needlework for bazaars and sales of work. Grandpa also sat here except when he wanted to smoke when he had to descend to the laundry to do so. No matter what the weather, he wore for this proceeding a velvet-trimmed jacket trimmed with cord and a little velvet porkpie hat which were later removed and replaced by his ordinary jacket before rejoining Grannie – so that her nostrils would not be affected by the obnoxious odour. The eldest daughter, Aunt Helen, sat in state in the drawing-room and did chrystoleum pictures and other handiwork.

Aunt Susan, with my mother Frances and Aunt Ethel, used the parlour, a tiny room which opened into the drawing-room if one wanted.

Francis, Fanny and Jane Espinasse were cousins of my grandfather Hypolite William Cornillon. Both families came from France to live in Edinburgh at the time of the Revolution. Francis was a writer and a journalist and was well thought of in literary circles in Edinburgh. He was connected with the *Edinburgh Courant*, a newspaper of the time. One of his books was *Literary Recollections*. He was a friend of Thomas and Jane Carlyle, and is mentioned in the book I have of her letters. Fanny and Jane added to their small income by teaching and they ran a little school together where my mother and her sisters had their early schooling. Jane also went as governess to titled families.

I remember these two little old ladies very well indeed. They lived not far from my grandfather's house in Dundonald Street and were constantly in and out. Fanny was a typical French 'marquise' type – very aristocratic looking with a pompadour of snow-white hair, keen black eyes and a full oval face with a rather pouting lower lip. Jane was tiny and not so distinguished looking. Both were of strong character.

Miss Brodie, the sewing woman, occupied this room when she came to make dresses for Grannie and the young ladies. She must have been a character by all accounts. She exclaimed that 'I canna mak dresses for Miss Edith [Henderson, friend of the family], she's as flat's a reid herrin'.' Another time – 'This machine'll no work the day … Yer Ma must have bin rammin' things through it agin.' One day when Mother was eating a pear in her company, Brodie remarked, 'That's a nice pear you're eatin!' 'Yes', agreed mother. 'Aye, and likely there'll be three to the poond?' Mother agreed once more. 'Aye, an' they'll be a shillin' a poond?' 'Yes', once more. 'Then,' with great emphasis, 'that's fowerpence you're eatin'!'

The household when my mother was a child consisted of the cook Ellen – affectionately known as Wee Ellen – the house-tablemaid Annie, laundrymaid Reid and nurses Mamie and Mame, younger sisters of Ellen who all came from Wick in Caithness. [Both Ellen and Annie stayed with my grandmother until her death, giving her over forty years of devoted service.] The laundry was all done at home, work commencing at five each Monday morning, so that the washing was finished by breakfast time; the mangling was done with a box mangle which I was taken to see by Ellen when I was older. The sheets and tablecloths were laid out on the large box and the roller with a boxful of stones to weigh it down was trundled from one end to the other. If any article did not pass muster with Grannie, it had to be done again – 'I could not ask Mr Cornillon to wear that!', she would say.

I used to be taken down the dark curling stairs of stone lit permanently by one tiny fishtail gas jet to visit Ellen in her sanctum, the kitchen. The kitchen was bright and light but the rest below was permanently dark, lit only from a narrow area in front. I think the maid's room did have a window. Coal was in cellars on this level and had to be carried up in scuttles to the rooms above.

The bathroom was in a dressing-room attached to my grandparents' bedroom. The lavatory had no window: when one wished to call there one groped in, found a box of matches tied by a string to the gas-jet and lit up. One could not be in a hurry and children always had to have an adult in attendance.

Mother and I used to visit about twice a year and at Christmas for the family gathering accompanied by Father. There was never a Christmas gathering at Barossa Place; I do not know why except that Mother was never on very friendly terms with my aunts and their meetings were very formal. I always used to enjoy these visits as we had a real fire in the evening in our bedroom, but my disappointment was great when I found it was not forthcoming in the morning; instead there was a curious gas fire in the bathroom like a beehive which gave out the minimum of heat. It was a type I have never seen before or since – a huge gas ring with a domed cover made of rough porous pottery and it had a ring of holes round the base – one could see the jets burning but felt no heat.

The hall and passages were all decorated in very dark colours so that in the passage it was always night-time as no light came from windows unless the pantry door happened to be left open. The house had a special aroma of its own, and to this day an old-fashioned musty smell brings a picture of it to my memory instantly.

Christmas Dinner was a great gathering. After my grandfather's death, Uncle Willie Wyse as senior son-in-law took the head of the table and carved. Grandmama at the other end served the Christmas and ice puddings. Dinner was at 6.30 p.m. to suit the young people. The menu was clear soup with macaroni stars, fish, entrée cutlets with mashed potato and vegetables, then turkey with all the trimmings or a second roast, usually pheasant, with fried potatoes, vegetable and crumbs, Christmas pudding or ice pudding, followed by a savoury (angels on horseback), dessert and wines. Instead of rolls, we had crispbread fingers called 'stangen' [German, sticks] served in little faggots tied with ribbon to match the table decorations.

After dinner, the uncles recited and sang, Aunt Susie played the piano and I my violin while others danced or sang. Tea was brought in at 9.30 p.m. with little cakes and biscuits, then the company dispersed. Usually there were Uncle Willie Wyse and Aunt Susie and Eddie, Uncle Arthur and Aunt Ethel with Maisie Gordon and later Kenneth, Pa and Ma and myself, Cousins Fanny and Jane Espinasse, and Peter Cousins, an old family friend. Cousin Fanny was stone deaf and brought her ear trumpet, a fearsome object about 18 inches long which she shot under the mouth of the person addressing her – my cousin Maisie christened it Cousin Fanny's Spittoon. Uncle Willie Wyse was a stockbroker and very well-off until by speculating too freely he 'crashed', and after that they moved to London.

A great interest when staying at Dundonald Street was to see the German bands come round to play and the barrel-organ grinders with a little monkey in uniform perched on top. The Newhaven fishwives, in their particular costume of striped blue and white petticoats with blue serge overskirts looped up and a shawl over head and shoulders and white shirt, carried their creels of fish on their shoulders by the aid of a leather strap on the forehead; Wee Ellen bargained for the fish as the house door opened onto steps from the street.

The dining-room was screened from passers-by by fine wire screens in a wooden frame bolted into the sides of the window frames – more suitable for office windows than a private house; I, naughty child, used to prick my initials in a corner of those screens, having discovered that a pin pushed between the mesh made a larger hole – I don't remember ever being found out, at least nothing was ever said to me.

Grannie died in 1913 and that ended my visits to Edinburgh, except for occasional ones to my Aunt Ethel at Ann Street – what Alisdair McEwan called 'that ghost-ridden street'. My Uncle Arthur and Aunt Ethel lived at number 30, over the Dean Bridge. This was a three-storey house in a terrace, with a fourth sunken storey for the kitchen: I never was allowed down there. The gate to the street and front garden was permanently locked, residents gained entrance with their keys but tradesmen and visitors rang a bell, then a maid came up from the basement and pressed down a stop in the front porch and lo! the gate opened. Tradesmen then went downstairs to the basement outer door to deliver their goods. This house was much lighter in its interior decoration, only the dining room being the usual sombre green colour. The stairs were circular, and these rooms being high, there was quite a climb to the top floor. From the nursery at the top of the house there was a grand view over Edinburgh towards the Forth. The back room on the ground floor was used first as a day nursery and later as a smoking-room – no one ever smoked in the ladies' drawing-room.

Uncle Willie Shaw and Aunt Nellie lived also in Ann Street on the opposite side from number 30 in what I recollect was a much smaller house. Uncle Willie Wyse and Aunt Susie lived not far away at 8 Dean Park Crescent and were always very kind to me, taking me to the theatre and to variety shows in Edinburgh when I was older. When they visited us or we met at Grannie's they would give me a generous 'tip'. I remember little of this house except that it was also very dark with dark red furnishings, as I only went there when quite a child and once in my teens to have dinner with Uncle Willie before going to the theatre. Another old friend of the family, Patrick Duick, contemporary with my parents,

played uncle and took me to the opera and gave me
the tiny pearl opera glasses in the green case for my
1911 birthday, when I was twenty-one.

My mother's only brother Charles died at the age
of twenty-one. I never saw him but I was told by my
mother that he had shot himself and I was never told
the circumstances.

2

Maids and Others

MY PARENTS started off married life with one general maid, Jane, who did all the work, cleaned the house, cooked and brought in the meals but did not wait at table. Her wages were between £18 and £24 per annum plus a length of material for a new print dress each New Year. She had two half-days until 10 p.m. off each week, one being on Sunday on alternate weekends. She might also attend church on Sunday morning if she wished.

When I appeared they had a nursemaid for me, first-named Annie, of whom I have no recollection but who no doubt did odd jobs and cleaned the nursery as well. She was followed by Jessie, a girl from Inverness whom I cannot picture but who I remember was nice to me and had the soft pure Inverness accent; she taught me my letters, and soon after, I was able to read as I was overheard reading something about the Matabele war from the paper.

She was followed when I was five by a dragon by the name of Mrs Watson, an old horror. I have a vivid recollection of running away round the nursery when she was trying to tie my petticoat bodice behind, I disliked her so much. One incident I remember was going for a walk to Scone village one afternoon. I used to be taken for walks of two to three miles or more. I wished to take my dolls' mailcart with me; this was made of wood and quite heavy and as we turned to come home one of the little wheels came off and it became impossible to push but Nurse refused to help me take it home as she had not wanted to bring it in the first place, so the little girl of five had to pull and drag the lamented mailcart home the best way she could; it was too heavy to carry. Retribution fell heavily upon me for my perverseness. She departed after a year and on leaving presented me with a child's religious book of the period, one of the hellfire gloomy kind for naughty children.

After Mrs Watson, a new regime was instituted – cook general and nurse housemaid, Kate and Jeannie Haggard. Kate had been with us for some time and her younger sister came along aged fifteen to be nurse housemaid. They received £18 and £12 per annum respectively; until Lloyd George introduced it (9d for employers and 4d for employees) there was no weekly insurance although I believe most families were insured for accidents to servants and the family doctor would attend the maids if ill. They were given a new print dress and aprons each New Year and had 'board' similar to mine, minus the cake and fruit at weekends. They remained with midday dinner when I was promoted to the evening meal and I think bread and butter formed the main part of their diet, with porridge for breakfast. Part of Jeannie's work was to look after me when mother was out and to take me for my daily walk. When her wages rose to £16 and Kate's to £20 maximum, both sisters departed to better themselves equipped with the experience they had gained with us. We started again with young ones at either £16 or £12 as a rule. They had two weeks' holiday in the year; they always came with us on our annual two weeks' holiday, but of course were working during that as we took a furnished house – a hotel was considered much too expensive and out of the question.

The maids wore long flowered print dresses for morning. The cook wore hers all day except on the housemaid's afternoon off when she changed into a black dress to be neat to open the door to afternoon callers. No one ever came on a social visit in the morning; any caller then came on a special errand of some sort.

The print floral dresses were very pretty in pale colours with a tiny floral sprig pattern – still to be seen in some old patchwork quilts. Usually the maids were given two lengths of this material each at New Year or Hairst Monday, the Scottish equivalent of England's Boxing Day. These dresses were made in the going style of skirt and boned bodice, but they were washable. I remember well the aroma and rustle on the mornings when the maids appeared in new prints – disappointingly this wore off after repeated washings. The dresses were always long and were pinned up if there was dirty work to be done necessitating kneeling.

In the morning, the dresses were covered by a very large white apron with a bib and they wore a little embroidered cambric cap like a cockscomb. After the midday meal the housemaid changed into a black serge dress (skirt and boned bodice) and wore a fine cambric apron with frills and bib and a more elaborate cap to match with streamers flowing down her back if she belonged to a 'grand' household; a pair of starched cuffs and a stiff collar like an Eton schoolboy's completed her costume. The cook did all the dirty work, such as scrubbing and blackleading grates, and wore a large hessian apron over her other things for protection. Only charwomen and the woman who came to do the washing wore coloured overalls over their clothing.

The only male retainer I can remember was James who took Grandpapa Cornillon to the office in the pony cart each day and would also be in attendance whenever the family went on holiday.

3

Clothing

Gude claes open all doors.
(Scots proverb)

A BABY in the 1880s wore an amazing amount of
clothing. First of all a flannel binder about 24
inches by 6 inches was wound round its body and
stretched firmly, leaving little expansion of the little
body after feeding. Next a flannel vest cut like a coat
bound with sarsenet [soft silk] ribbon and with ties for
fastening, and then a thick turkish nappy with a flannel
pilch [a triangular piece of flannel with a binding of
ribbon] over it was put on.

After these there was a flannel petticoat called a
barracoat. This had a sleeveless coat bodice and was
fastened with ribbon ties, the skirt part, which was
longer than the baby's legs, was edged with buttonhole
scallops. Over this a cambric embroidered petticoat was
tied at the back so that the infant had to be reversed

onto its tummy for this purpose. Finally the robe made of lawn, silk or cashmere also fastened at the back. The robe and petticoats were at least 30 inches from neck to hem, but the baby was 'shortened' at six months. A quilted bib of piqué [heavy, corded cotton fabric] or silk, for best occasions, was put on to protect the clothing from dribbles. This was fastened down in front with a silver brooch usually engraved with the word BABY. In the house the baby was wrapped as well in a large Shetland wool shawl, woollen bootees on its feet and frequently a triangle of scalloped cashmere as a head shawl.

Out of doors the baby wore a long carrying coat of cashmere edged with swan's down fur [similar to a strip of feather boa] – this usually had two or three graduated capes all edged with fur. Girl babies wore a cashmere bonnet much ruched and edged with fur and with another little cape at the neck edge to make sure no gap existed between bonnet and cloak. When very young and being still carried out, a silk veil was fixed over the unfortunate infant's face and wool mitts were tied onto the hands.

Boys wore a little pork pie hat of cashmere edged with fur and tied with broad ribbons. The baby was carried out for the first month of its life for a short time each day and the rest of the time it lay in its cot in the nursery. Babies were never left to sleep outside in the pram – this was only used to wheel them out for a short period.

After a child was born the mother was made to lie flat on her back for the first week, in the second week she was allowed to move a little and to sit up for a short time each day. In the third week she was allowed up for a little and in the fourth week she was able to go out a little with the baby and the hospital nurse in attendance. Then the hospital nurse departed and the mother coped with the baby with the aid of a children's nurse. Sometimes these were just motherly women who liked looking after children, others had had a course of training in child care, such as the Princess Christian nurses had, but as they commanded high salaries, they were only employed by the well-to-do.

Dummies were always used and a bone or ivory teething ring too. Bottle-fed babies had bottles like the one I have drawn with a small glass tube inside the bottle inserted in a cork and outside the bottle a long rubber tube ending in a teat with a bone 'stopper' [see plate section]. It must have been highly unhygienic, as it was impossible to turn the tube inside out for cleaning or to put a brush through the glass tube. Babies however could attend to their own feeding by means of such a bottle until they choked I presume. No solid food was given until the baby was nine months old then it was mostly sloppy and perhaps a rusk to chew. At three months the mixture was 6 ounces, half milk, half water; by nine months 8 ounces of full milk was reached. As a matter of fact all my children were fed in this way and thrived on it.

At six months the baby clothes were dispensed with, but the clothing was much the same in quantity, the stitched binder being replaced at about three months by a woven one. I was walked out in a very high bassinet pram until I was about three when I was promoted to a wooden mail-cart; this was a wooden arrangement with two seats back to back, solid tires and no springs.

As a little girl I wore in winter wool combinations, a Rational corset bodice (a type of Liberty bodice but made in thick white corset material), ribbed woollen stockings in black or sometimes gingery tan colour, a flannel petticoat with cambric bodice, a blue and white swansdown [fine woollen material] striped petticoat on top with a cambric bodice both fastened with tapes and buttons at the back. In winter I had swansdown knickers buttoned onto the buttons of the Rational corset bodice, a dress of some thick woollen material and a cambric pinafore on top of all. Sealskin coats were very fashionable and worn over the dress with a perky little hat.

For parties I was allowed to discard the flannel petticoat and had a cambric one with embroidered cotton frills in place of the striped one, with knickers of cambric to match – these were also summer wear. One party dress I had was of green shantung [coarse silk] with long sleeves, and a lace collar and cuffs made by my grannie. Another was of velveteen, another of pale blue cashmere smocked, another of smoked crème silk, and a white muslin over pale green silk.

The best perhaps was a gorgeous pink silk dress with silk stockings with open-work ankles and pink satin shoes to match. When Jeannie was called in to see me in my glory dressed for the party, she exclaimed 'Eh, Miss Frances, you'll be the belly of the Ball!'

In summer outdoors I wore buttoned shoes, in winter heavier shoes with long buttoned felt gaiters. I never remember wearing socks and my recollection of any clothing was that I felt acutely uncomfortable especially on Sundays when clean combinations were put on me. I itched from their scratching all day. Summer brought some relief with silk and wool vests and cotton stockings.

At about seven I was promoted to coats and skirts with Viyella blouses in spring and cotton ones in winter. Mother had a scarlet frieze coat with a blue velvet collar made for me which was similar to a coat of father's. I wore it over a blue serge dress topped with a Balmoral bonnet with a goose claw badge and I liked the outfit very much until some rude children shouted after me 'Eh, look at the lassie in her brither's bonnet!' as a Balmoral bonnet was a male headpiece.

Summer dresses were made of Viyella for cooler days and checked and striped gingham for only really hot days. There were no cardigans or pullovers then so it was a coat of some sort on top for more warmth. The first cardigans appeared when I was about thirteen or fourteen, jumpers a good deal later. Ladies wore knitted spencers [short woollen jackets] under their blouses.

Up to about 1896–98 women wore dresses which were in two pieces – a long skirt to the ground of plain wool or silk material, trimmed with lace or braid according to the occasion it was to be worn, and a bodice, tight-fitting with leg o'mutton sleeves and boned quite heavily.

The hem of the skirt was edged with brush braid to prevent it from wearing. Nothing was washable. Blouses came in later and these were more like a man's shirt with high starched collars and cuffs. Combinations were worn, woollen or cotton according to season and cotton knickers and a petticoat from the waist of calico or moire [watered silk] with frills which rustled as the wearer walked about.

Black stockings, cotton or wool, were worn with outdoor button boots in winter and shoes in summer; shoes and boots were usually made to measure especially for choosy customers as there was not the range of styles and sizes we have today. For dances and parties stockings and white satin shoes were dyed to match the dress. One never wore a soft bedroom type shoe except in the bedroom or bathroom.

When going out a short jacket of heavy cloth was worn over the dress – much in the style of the dress bodice; it could be of sealskin with a matching hat perched on top of tightly dressed hair. Hats were often of heavy felt in winter trimmed with velvet, feathers, flowers or French knot bugles [bead trimming] and specially made for 'Modom' by a milliner.

Of course women did not exert themselves in those days but even so their clothes must have got very stuffy as only their underclothes were washable. Corsets were very stiff-boned and had only a life of about six months as the whalebones broke and dug into one. I remember the acute discomfort as I came into wearing this type of garment in my teens – very different from the Rational bodice. I cannot remember my mother ever wearing a mackintosh, only carrying an umbrella in case she was caught out in the rain. If it was wet and one was out, a cab was taken to convey one home. It was not necessary in the ordinary course of events for women to go out shopping as tradesmen sent a boy daily for orders and later the goods were delivered by the same boy on foot carrying a large covered basket or in a van if it was a large order. The baker's van called daily with the bread. So the only shopping that had to be attended to personally was for clothing or to visit the library or the post and the like, which was reserved for fine days. Women therefore spent a lot of time in their homes and must have suffered from boredom as all the housework was done for them – they only ordered the meals and organised the work of the house.

Much time was spent in embroidery and making children's clothes – adults apparel was too complicated for a home dressmaker, so a 'little woman' dressmaker was found for the making of everyday wear. Mother made a lot of my clothes. For important garments one patronised a good clothing shop such as McEwans in Perth, to have things made, where everything (as later at Arnisons of Penrith) was 'the very best'. Ready-made clothes were considered non-U [not socially acceptable] and in any case they were very poor quality.

In summer, clothing for women was similar except for being made of lighter weight fabrics and the coat was less heavy. Hats were of straw, still elaborately trimmed. Parasols with frills and feather boas were carried and worn in summer – everything was very ornate.

Men's clothing was much the same as nowadays except of course the styles were different. Much more formal clothing was worn. Businessmen and doctors for instance wore frock coats and tall silk hats. A Norfolk jacket and knickers were worn for fishing and country wear; the jacket had pockets with a box pleat down the middle so that they were roomy; a belt was stitched with the coat with a loose tab and buckle for fastening; the breeches were only slightly baggy. A high stiff collar was worn even with this suit, knee stockings with laced boots and gaiters and usually a fore and aft cap, Sherlock Holmes style, or a very small tweed cap like a schoolboy's with a small peak, completed the outfit.

For tennis and boating white flannels and a highly coloured blazer (if he did not possess a school or college one) were worn with a straw boater with striped ribbon to match the blazer.

Inverness capes were worn as topcoats in the more country districts. This cape was a very long overcoat with half-capes in front of the coat to cover the arms. In town, a 'covert' coat of heavy 'face' cloth (not turkish towelling, but a smooth felt-like material) was often worn or a black coat of serge if one was a business or professional man. Trousers were 'drainpipe' and in fact all men's clothing looked rather tight for them and badly cut even in aristocratic circles. Bowler hats were daily business wear and my grandfather wore a felt hat in the form of a rather low-crowned top hat. Not until about 1910 did men's clothing become more comfortable looking and easy fitting. Three-piece grey flannel suits for summer came in then to be followed later by the tweed sports jacket and grey flannel 'bags'.

Mourning clothes were worn for one full year, black for six months and then grey or purple depending on the nearness of the relative for six months. Widows wore 'weeds' until they too died, if they were elderly; younger women would wear black with crepe bands for a year and then black or dark grey for six months. For less near relatives one modified the mourning but it was never less than six months. When Queen Victoria and Edward VII died the entire country wore black for six months without exception. Social etiquette was very rigid. I was very upset as Mother took my new and lovely yellow spring suit and dyed it black to meet the requirement but it went a horrid dingy green instead. Hearses were adorned with urns and black ostrich feathers and black horses had plumes of feathers sprouting from their headbands.

In the winter of 1908 I 'put my hair up' and 'came out'. My dress for the first ball was white – 'de rigueur' in those days for a debutante, made of crêpe-de-chine, in semi-Georgian style, long to the ground with a little train which was looped up by a ribbon loop over my arm when I danced. I had a second white dress that winter too also in high-waisted Regency style in a soft satin. No make-up, not even a discreet dab of powder was allowed.

My second year out, I had a black dress added to my evening wardrobe and every year following a new dress for the main dance of the season, the last year's dress being considered all right for the smaller affairs. I remember the lovely dress of pale blue and sweet-pea lavender with bands of dull bead trimming in blue, darker lavender and gold and a gold cord with tassels round my waist and shoes to match. Another was black satin with dull gold trimming in tunic style; another, black with pink and white chiffon bodice trimmed with pearly beads and silver sequins. Two others I remember were a soft white satin dress with a black lace over-tunic and a sky-blue soft silk brocade with a fichu-lace bodice fastened in front with a strip of cherry ninon and a small bunch of cherry velvet fruits. One dress I hated was made for me by a dressmaker: it had a pale blue taffeta underdress and the top was a sort of canvas material in crème [sic] which was open enough to show the blue through but was thick and rather clumsy trimmed with bands of blue and white embroidery to match. All these dresses were long to the ground, short dance dresses came in with World War One.

At concerts and the theatre no one ever went to the best seats and dress circle in anything but full evening dress with which one wore a special evening cloak or coat – one's ordinary day or fur coat would just not have done. When one compares theatre and concert audiences today a lot of the glamour has gone.

4

Holidays and Transport

THERE was very little going away from home up to the time of World War One; the weekend habit had not taken on generally but was confined to society people as it had been started by Edward VII. Holidays in my childhood were few and for people like ourselves usually confined to the annual month in the country or the seaside; my parents did not care for a seaside holiday so we went instead to places near a loch or river where my father could get fishing and perhaps golf, although this was not required so much as he played regularly at home.

We did not go far afield, mostly to places in Perthshire – Crieff, St Fillans, Loch Ard. We spent two holidays at St Fillans, once when I was four and later when I was seven. This was in early September and my earliest recollection of the annual holiday was of a little very dark house we rented. There I made a snake of burrs and left it on the kitchen floor where it caused great consternation when Kate and Jeannie returned from an outing – in the dim light they mistook it for a real one and there were cries of alarm, much to my amusement. We took bed linen and silver and stores, as small local shops were not then stocked with more than basic requirements; the maids came with us and had their own two weeks' holiday later at separate times so we were not left without domestic staff. Loch Awe and Loch Goilhead in Argyll were both favourite holiday places.

In 1897 we had a famous holiday at Kingussie when aunts and uncles and friends joined and foregathered in various rented furnished houses there for a month. Operations began in Edinburgh, where a large saloon compartment carriage was chartered and added to the usual train from Edinburgh to Perth, where it arrived complete with Uncle and Aunt Wyse plus their son Eddie and their two maids, Uncle Arthur and Aunt Ethel with Maisie and Gordon and nurse and maids. The saloon was uncoupled at Perth and shunted and joined to the Highland train and Father and Mother and I and our two maids joined the glad throng. My cousin Maisie insisted that we were travelling in a balloon. At Kingussie we split up and went to our respective furnished houses. The men, who had only two weeks' holiday from business, spent their days fishing and were joined by various men friends; they usually returned for a few days at the end of the month to round off the holiday with their families.

The mothers devoted their time to the children and running the household as at home. A pony was hired and rides were taken each day or it pulled a governess cart; it was very stout and not a very comfortable ride for short fat legs. It was also very lazy and when driven had a habit of standing obstinately still at every inn and public house on the way – someone had to get out and pull it past when it would proceed on its way until we came to another.

Eddie lost a tooth when we were all playing under the dining-room table one day and went home in a great rage and alarm saying 'You've knocked it down my throat, you dirty brutes' – this aged nine! However, to everyone's relief the maids found the tooth when sweeping the floor the next morning; in those days this job was done with a short sweeping brush and dustpan – no vacuum cleaners. I have a feeling I did not enjoy this holiday very much, being rather overborne by my cousins Eddie and Maisie who played two to one.

I think it was the next year in 1898 that we went to Loch Awe in September; we had some visitors – Corrie Chisholme and Nancy Buist – and I learned to row a boat. We went again to the same house in 1905 and I remember being surprised to find how small the rooms and the house appeared as my memory was of a very large house.

The last family holiday when we rented a house was spent at Loch Goil. After that Father took his holidays golfing and fishing on his own and Mother and I went together to Loch Goil each year until about 1910 when I went by myself. Mother loathed going from home and remained there to enjoy her garden. In 1908 a white whale was washed up and beached on the shore of the loch and drew large crowds. Other years I visited Liverpool (1910), Ireland with Bar Scott, and Epsom to the races.

Every spring in early May until my Grandfather Cornillon died in 1897 we used to stay with them at Loch Ard where he and Grannie rented a house for a period and had their daughters and families to stay. We went by train from Perth to Aberfoyle; railway fares were very small; one could go to Edinburgh return for 5 shillings and even up to about 1910 one could travel return from Perth to London for under £3 third class. Of course there were no steam-heated trains in winter – one was provided with foot warmers which were two-foot-long metal containers about 10 inches wide and 3 inches deep covered with carpeting and filled with boiling water and brought along the train on porters' trolleys at the beginning of the journey. One always took a travelling rug or hired one for a nominal sum from the railway.

I do not know how people travelling long distances fared as the heat could only have lasted a moderate time from the warmers. There were no corridors in trains, no dining cars, no toilets: one got off at certain stops for food and toilets. There were smoking carriages; the rest were non-smoking and Ladies Only.

[The last Ladies Only compartments were taken off the East Anglian Line in 1977.]

At Aberfoyle James met us with the governess cart and drove us the few miles to the house. This was near the loch and Grandpapa used to fish every day in company with his sons-in-law. I can remember being there with my Uncle Arthur's family and Uncle Willie Wyse, so the house must have been a large one to accommodate us all. Family prayers were said and read morning and night. Grannie used to take me out to the stable to give the pony lumps of sugar. Some cottage children lived near by and I remember a small boy having his hair trimmed by his mama with an inverted pudding basin on his head so she could cut it in a straight line. There was a lovely garden to play in, or we went fowling on the loch in a boat if Grandpapa did not require it for fishing, or we went for drives around the country in the pony cart. After 1897 these happy holidays ended.

After she was a widow, Grannie used to rent a house at Loch Goil for two or three months and have her daughters and grandchildren to stay with her for visits of about two weeks. The first of these holiday homes was a flat at the top of a large house let off by the owners who lived in the main house all the year round. The flat was entered by an outside stair and so was completely separate from the main house. The house belonged to a Mrs Hamilton who had two daughters and sons who came down from Glasgow each weekend, as did most of the families who had summer houses at Loch Goil and town houses for the winter in Glasgow. This Mrs Hamilton and her daughters were the grandmother and aunts of Hamish Hamilton the publisher whom I remember as Jimmy Hamilton, a small rather 'enfant terrible' resplendent at the kirk on Sundays in kilt, black velvet jacket and lace ruffles. He had a very pronounced Glesca' accent.

In later years, Grannie was able to rent a villa for the whole summer, May to October, but not always the same one until finally she went every year to one called Braefoot which belonged to a family called Jevons. One of the sons was a professor whose subject was geology. There was a large library in this house in which I was allowed to browse to my heart's content on rainy days, of which, during some of our July visits, there were many. The west coast was renowned for its wet summers and midges.

When I was older I went by myself to stay with Grannie for much longer periods and it was there I met the Jellett family from Dublin: Willie and Janet and their family of four girls, Maisie, Bay (Dorothea), Babbin and Elizabeth Henrietta. Janet had been a Miss Stokes, sister of Dr Henry Stokes of the Rotunda Hospital in Dublin and of Adrian Stokes who lost his life in research on yellow fever, in his own laboratory, shortly after World War One.

Mrs Jellett's aunt Izzie Watson had her own summer residence there. Her son Jack was a violinist and was

PLATE I. Frances Emily Hill Rimington

PLATE 2. Frances EH Rimington, aged 7, and Edith Leslie, aged 6.

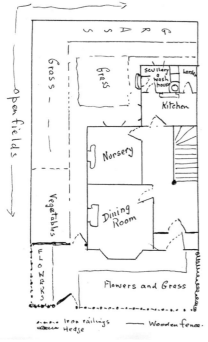

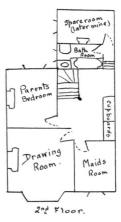

PLATE 3. Plan of 8 Rosemount Place, Perth

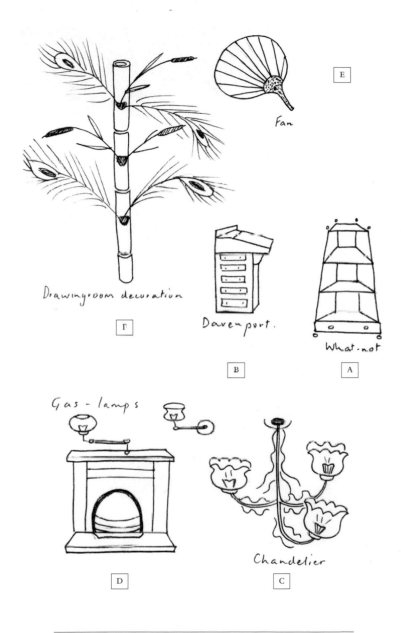

Fan

E

Drawingroom decoration

Г

Davenport.

B

What-not

A

Gas - lamps

Chandelier

D

C

PLATE 4. a. What-not b. Davenport c. Chandelier d. Gaslights
e. Palm leaf fan-decoration f. Bullrushes in a length of bamboo-decoration

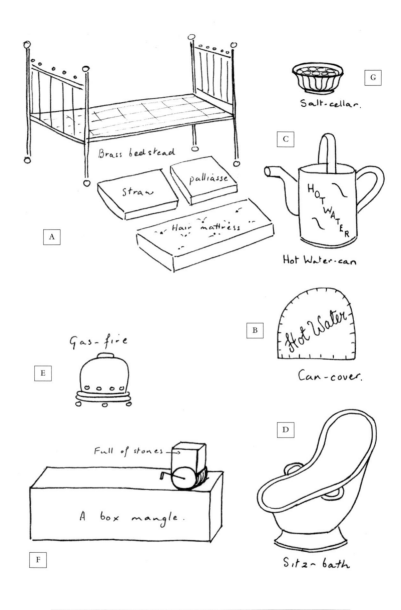

Salt-cellar.

Brass bedstead

Straw palliasse

Hair mattress

Hot Water-can

Gas-fire

Hot Water Can-cover.

Full of stones →

A box mangle.

Sitz-bath

PLATE 5. a. Bedstead and mattress b. Can-cover c. Hot water-can
d. Sitz-bath e. Gas-fire f. Box mangle g. Salt-cellar

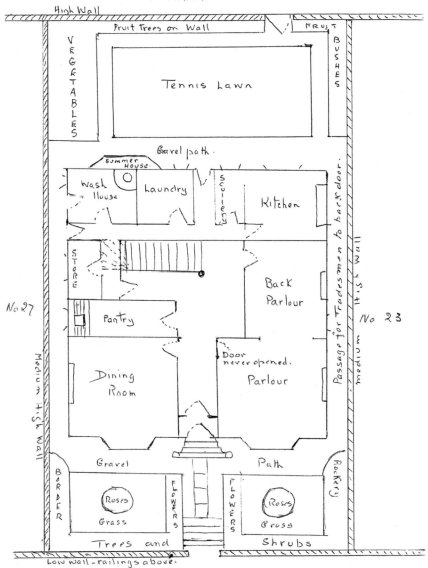

PLATE 6. Plan of 25 Barossa Place, Perth,
the home of John Thomas

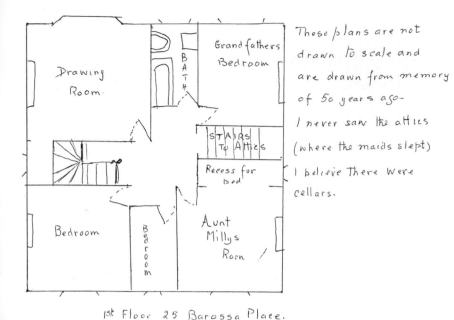

Drawing Room.

Grandfathers Bedroom

BATH

STAIRS To Attics

Recess for Bed

Bedroom

Bedroom

Aunt Millys Room

These plans are not drawn to scale and are drawn from memory of 50 years ago. I never saw the attics (where the maids slept) I believe there were cellars.

1st Floor 25 Barossa Place.

PLATE 7. First-floor plan of Barossa Place, Perth

PLATE 8. Aunt Carrie, friend, Amy Leslie and
Edith 'Tootie' Leslie, Barossa Place, Perth

PLATE 9. *top* (*a*). Edith Leslie, Amy Leslie and Frances Rimington
above (*b*). Elevenses in the parlour at No. 25

One Floor down are the Kitchen, larders _ scullery maids bedroom and in the double-sunk_ the laundry and cellars_ Everything had to be carried up by the maids_ coals, meals, etc. The common stair went up to two more flats.

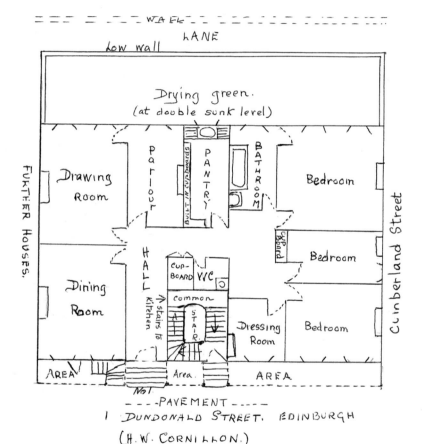

PLATE 10. Plan of 1 Dundonald Street, Edinburgh

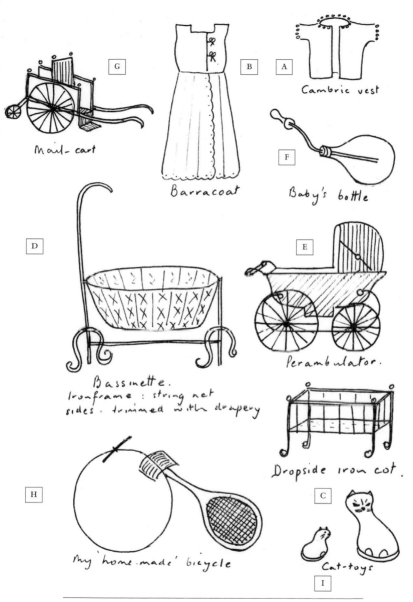

G Mail-cart

B Barracoat

A Cambric vest

F Baby's bottle

D Bassinette.
Ironframe : string net
sides. trimmed with drapery

E Perambulator.

Dropside iron cot.

H My 'home-made' bicycle

C / I Cat-toys

PLATE 11. a. Cambric vest b. Barracoat c. Dropside iron cot
d. Bassinette, iron frame, string sides, trimmed with drapery e. Perambulator
f. Baby's bottle g. Mail-cart h. My 'home-made' bicycle i. Cat-toys

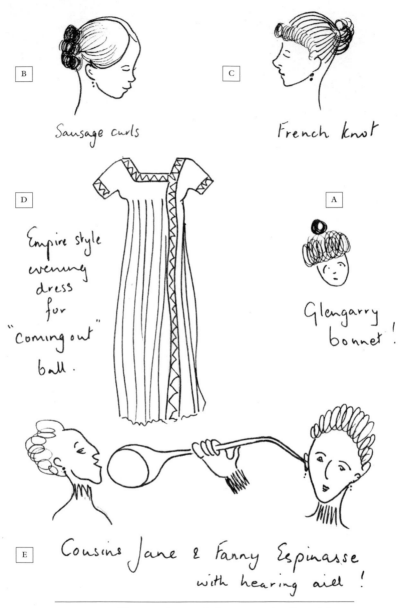

B

Sausage curls

C

French knot

D

Empire style evening dress for "coming out" ball.

A

Glengarry bonnet !

E

Cousins Jane & Fanny Espinasse with hearing aid !

PLATE 12. a. Glengarry bonnet b. Sausage curls c. French knot
d. Empire style evening dress for 'coming-out' ball.
e. Cousins Jane and Fanny Espinasse with hearing aid

PLATE 13. Frances Rimington as a flapper, *c.* 1905

PLATE 14. Diana Brisco Malik (née Rimington)

PLATE 15. John Hill Thomas, Captain 4th V.B. Blackwatch R.H., 1900–1907

violin professor at the Dublin School of Music, the post his cousin Bay Jellett now holds. His sister Eileen married Ralph Cusack, father of the garden expert Ralph, who wrote the strange book *Cadenza*.

A lot of very nice friends lived here and I think that my holidays here were amongst the happiest days of my life. The factor of the 'big house', Drumsynie Lodge, was Mr Macfarlane who had a very large Victorian mama-type wife. She was quite the plainest woman I think I have ever seen, but so kind and hospitable and cheerful and full of humour – she lived to be ninety-nine. They also had a family of daughters, Jennie May, Harriet (Hatty) – plain as her mama – and a much younger sister, Winifred, who was a little younger than myself; we had many boating picnics and swimming with these friends. Their home was on the far side of the loch from the village.

On Sundays they rowed (wet or fine) in their boat across to church, but this was the only boat outing they were permitted on the Sabbath and no picnics, although they were pleased to welcome friends to tea on Sunday who came by boat from the opposite side. We also played golf on the little nine-hole course in front of Drumsynie Lodge. Did I say nine holes? There were nine official holes but hundreds of rabbit holes down which one's ball often rolled, and one went round the course with a good supply in one's bag. If the ball had gone farther down a rabbit hole than could be easily hooked out with a club, one did not bother as next day it was almost certain to be found again by Benjamin Bunny.

We used to fish in the little rivers, being devoured by midges as a rule. The Macfarlanes had some very nice cousins who came every year from Bournemouth, called Ballantine. They all joined in these activities so picnics were on a grand scale. We lunched or tea'd or suppered out most days, either with our individual family groups or on occasions all families combined. Sometimes we camped out all night but this was weather permitting of course.

May and June were the best months and September and early October too. I was there in each of these months in various years. July and August were the wet months. Betty Henderson, an old friend, ten years or more older than myself, was a very fine walker and swimmer; she scandalised my old grannie by bathing with her fiancé, both attired in a high-to-the-neck-down-to-the-knees style of bathing suit.

Tea parties with competitions and prizes were frequent and much enjoyed in the manner of Cranford. Drives to neighbouring places in the afternoon were another of Grannie's treats to visitors in a small open wagonette with a couple of horses. On the very steep gradients the younger members of the party got out and walked to ease the weight for the horses. Then home to high tea if we had not taken tea with us. Tea out of doors was a fire and kettle affair – no thermos tea in those days. First job for the youngsters was to fetch kindling and wood and the grown-ups lit and attended the fire and made the tea. Yes, we had plenty of simple enjoyable pleasure with no thought of war until 1914.

In 1914 I had been on a motor tour round Argyll-shire and the lochs with Mrs Jos, an old friend. Cars were open then and one wore a dustcoat, veils and goggles as the roads were very rutted, uneven and dusty. When war broke out I was staying with the Jelletts and Mother wrote commanding my instant return home. However, to my joy Mrs Jellett wrote and calmed Mother's panic and I was able to finish my holiday. I went once again in 1916 and then never again until 1932, when I spent a few days there and then for the last time in 1937 when Susan and I stayed there for a couple of weeks and I was amazed to find how little the place and people had changed since 1916. I was remembered by the blacksmith and postmistress after twenty years.

With the Jelletts we gave entertainments to help the War Fund: concerts and pantomimes. One summer the Jelletts organised a concert in aid of a local charity with Romberg's celebrated Toy Symphony in which the toys were played by local worthies. Another year their children and friends produced a pantomime; the chauffeur at the 'big house' did noble work in providing light with the large lamps from his employers' Rolls Royce car.

Each year the Local Volunteers gave a dance to which all the gentry were bidden. The men all wore the kilt and scarlet mess jacket – the blacksmith looked especially resplendent in his kilt and was a fine dancer, as were most of the village men. The dance was held in the village hall next door to the hotel and my guess is that the men popped in there for a quick one between dances – ladies never. No saloon bars in those days. They asked the young ladies of the various families to dance, and when each dance was finished one was returned to one's seat at the side of the dance floor and left with a bow. At home between 2 and 3 a.m. hearing the first cock crow and the clink-clonk of oars breaking the night silence – some revellers returning by boat – no cars or horse transport at that time of night. Happy carefree days indeed.

One year Aunt Izzie took me and Maisie Jellett to Glasgow for the night to go to a concert given by Carreiro who was a fine lady pianist of those days. It shows how inexpensive things were then for us to be able to do this. A few shillings for the steamer return fare to Greenock and again for the railway fare to Glasgow, the evening meal, bed and breakfast at an hotel – I think the whole cost came to under a pound; Aunt Izzie had got the tickets for us all. She was a character; she bathed every day early morning right up to the end of October and her pug dog was forcibly held by the scruff of his neck and tail and soused.

There were steamers on both Loch Goil and Loch Awe and of course 'doon the Watta', a favourite outing down the Clyde by steamer. On one occasion I remember a flustered mama towards the end of a trip with a trying family announced, ' I cam' oot for plesha an' I havna haad it!'

When I stayed with the Jelletts we had a lot of music together, playing Beethoven's symphonies etc. There were Geraldine Fitzgerald, Bay, Maisie and Mother (two pianos), Jock and Eileen (cello). One summer we had a moonlight musical party in boats with Chinese lanterns. All those who could sing and play were rounded up by Janet Jellett, who rehearsed us. One fine night, without warning anyone, we set out in boatloads, rowing slowly and quietly past all the houses where the occupants came out to greet us and listen. The loch was flat calm and the sound floated out marvellously. After an hour or so, we returned to a lovely supper at the Jelletts. Two other families, cousins to the family Hamilton, took part in this. I can see them all in a mental picture but I cannot remember their surname for the life of me; one mother was called by Mrs Jellett 'Mrs Flet Het' as she had the flat 'A' pronunciation of Glasgow and used to say of somebody she wore 'a flet het'. All nice kindly friendly people with traces of Victorianism still clinging to their ways of doing.

5

Schooling

I STARTED lessons with Mother at the age of five: reading and writing, simple arithmetic, geography, history from 'Little Arthur's England', piano lessons and French. In 1897 when I was six and a half, until I was nearly ten, I had a daily governess, Miss Jemima Logie. I used to go to the little school her sister had in their home once a week for dancing lessons. There was a queer old dragon of a woman to teach us who was very bad-tempered. One day she seemed very queer indeed before I began lessons, and while Mother and Miss Logie were talking, I was sent out of the room but I am afraid I eavesdropped and learned that the dancing mistress had evidently had a drop too much, being 'disposed' to put her lips to a bottle like Sairey Gamp apparently. I continued with these dancing lessons and do not remember any further incidents.

In September 1900, Miss Logie was succeeded by Miss Alice Carnegie, who taught me all the subjects including languages, needlework, drawing (no painting), piano theory and harmony until I was fifteen and a half in July 1906. Dancing proceeded at a class given by a little man and his sister who came over from Edinburgh each Saturday morning. I cannot recollect his name now but he was a rather celebrated exponent of ballroom dancing and at this time it was 'the thing' to be taught by him.

After Miss Carnegie's reign I was sent to the Westlands School in Scarborough for two years until July 1908 and returned home 'finished'. The houses in which it was are still standing at the top of the Valley Road but are now I believe offices or maybe boarding houses. I believe that the school was let as summer visitors' quarters in the holidays and I often wondered if our sheets and towels were used for the purpose.

The headmistress Emma Wood was a bit of a dragon and one was rather in awe of her. She had a younger sister, rather fat and flabby, who was nicknamed The Lamb. I never knew why, unless it was meant to contrast with Miss Wood. I didn't like her much but had little to do with her. The music mistresses were Miss Compere (a very *grande dame* indeed) and Miss Pearce who looked like an innocent choirboy with glasses. Miss Hodgkinson taught English and was very religious – I recollect hearing her weeping all through the night as her room was next to the one where I slept, after she heard of the death of a small nephew from appendicitis. Miss Gibb 'took' hockey and taught geography – she was a tailor-made type with greying hair and startling cold china-blue eyes. She followed as geography mistress an awful woman called Miss Kemp who had a perpetual cold and always-filthy handkerchiefs. She used to 'help' the milk puddings with a knife. After her class ended she once said, 'Gels, the joraffy for Toosday will be the Noo York rilewiys'. Mademoiselle Odette Prunier de St André taught us French and a dear old Fräulein German. If we were feeling disinclined to work in her classes, one of us would bring up the subject of 'der Mittel-alter' (Middle Ages) and Fräulein was off hot on the scent with most entertaining histories of this and that in the period – very interesting but not calculated to gain us progression in the language.

Our uniform. We wore long skirts and white shirt blouses; only on gym days did we wear our tunics and were obliged to wear them over our skirts until class time when we discarded the skirts. From time to time gym displays were given to parents but the only man ever allowed to attend these was the school doctor – it was not seemly that we should be seen with skirts only to the knee by any other male, even the fathers. Games of hockey and tennis were played in long skirts.

When I began to learn the violin in 1898 I was taught by Miss Janey Burton, one of three sisters who had a girls' boarding and day school in Blackfriars House near the North Inch in Perth. Her sister Ella played the cello. I went to the school for my lessons and my memory of it was that it was a very dark house (I believe it was once part of a monastery). When I had been learning for about a year, I was allowed to join the school orchestra and can picture myself sitting in the back row of the second violins playing 'oom-papa – oom-papa' in the Cachincha from the *Gondoliers* and being scared when Miss Ella ticked off one of the bigger girls for passing a note to another girl during the rehearsal.

Pupils' concerts were given once or twice a year. My first effort was 'An Idyll' by Nans Sitt which was a piece all in dotted minims, with no doubt an elaborate waltz accompaniment. On returning home, my pride was lowered by being told off by my mother for using only niggly little bows instead of the whole length. On another occasion I played a potpourri of Scotch Airs and the Waltz from *Faust*. I played at various small concerts such as entertainments for infirmary patients and women prisoners at Perth General Prison. I also played from the age of twelve in orchestras for the local choral societies, of the cathedral and one of the parish churches.

In 1900, the school was given up and the Miss Burtons left Perth. I went for lessons to Herr Gottlieb Feurberg who had a Scottish wife, two little boys, Ian and Rudolf, and a little girl Nesta. I progressed well with this teacher and by the age of twelve was able to play solos with the pupils' orchestra augmented by the adult pupils like my Aunt Caroline and the aforesaid

Claire Fleming and two brothers of my friend Alice Martin and herself.

I continued to study with this master until I went to school in Scarborough where I gave up piano and concentrated on the violin, being taught by William Henry Cass who died there in 1962 aged ninety-four. He was a good master, but I resumed lessons with Herr GF after leaving school in 1908 and continued until 1914 when at the outbreak of war the poor man was interned as being German although his sons were fighting for us and Ian was killed. I never saw Gottlieb Feurberg again; he went back to Germany after release from internment.

After a time the Perth Orchestral Society was formed out of the pupils' orchestra, under the title of the St Johnston's Orchestra, with GF as conductor. Several adults and pupils joined and concerts were given two or three times a year in the City Hall. These were always social occasions with everyone in the best seats in full evening dress and opera cloaks, and white kid gloves. As also in the theatre now opened in Perth, the Dress Circle was the Dress Circle and no one would have been allowed to enter improperly dressed. World War One put paid to all this formality, rather to our loss in some ways – a bit of gracious living gone.

Mother was always very fearful that I should come to some harm away from home. In 1909 when I left school she would not agree to my going to Germany to study music, and later, after it was arranged for me to go to the Royal Academy of Music, the war came and put a stop to that too, sadly.

6

Entertainments

Music hath charms ...
(Shakespeare)

For the first ten years of my life I was a Victorian. In the winter of 1895–96 occurred the Great Frost when the River Tay was frozen over solid for several weeks in February. High junketings took place, skating and carnivals, and an ox was roasted for supper picnics. Golf was played on the North Inch with red-painted balls to show up on the snowy frosty ground. My Nurse Jessie took me for a walk along a stretch of the river and I walked under the bridge – there was only one across the river in those days; Queen Victoria opened the new Victoria Bridge in 1900.

As far as I can remember these wintry conditions lasted about three weeks before the first thaw came and then an avalanche of burst pipes was followed by a plumbers' harvest.

The winters seemed much harder then, because after this I was taught to skate and remember doing so for quite long periods every winter. We had to walk about a couple of miles to a pond artificially flooded for the purpose. There was a hut where tea and Bovril were sold and certain eatables, but Mother and I usually took our own; one could hire skates and there were chairs like deck chairs on runners to which one could cling while still unsteady on one's feet.

Curling bonspiels were held annually in which my father played. All and sundry, country gentlemen, farmers and the like, mingled together with many old men wearing Balmoral (tam o'shanter style) bonnets and checked plaids wrapped around them for warmth in place of a top coat.

When I was older some friends at Hellyland gave a wonderful party on the ice and there was a supper marquee and the place was all lit with fairy lamps and Japanese lanterns, but alas, a rapid thaw set in in the midst of our enjoyment and we had to end the party sooner than we would otherwise have done owing to a couple of inches of water on top of the ice.

One summer when I was about four or five I remember seeing balloons being sent up from some fête being held on the North Inch that Mother and I watched from her bedroom window. The balloons were figures of people and I think they were filled with gas to become airborne and gradually disintegrated, much to my grief.

Queen Victoria's Diamond Jubilee was in 1897, marked by gifts of mugs and silver medals to children to commemorate the event – I don't know what happened to mine.

About this time I was given my first bicycle; before this I had made myself one with a hoop and an old tennis racquet on which I careered about hobby-horse fashion with the hoop stick tied on as handle bars and an old magazine as saddle – necessity being the mother of invention. The great day came when the real bicycle and I were taken to a photographer's in Crieff. Why I was always taken to Crieff to be photographed I don't know, unless he was especially good with children. The first time I was taken at four I protested loudly that I didn't want to be 'puttagraffed' but the deed was somehow quietly accomplished and I came away triumphantly exclaiming 'I never was puttagraffed!' I must have had some rooted objection to prominence because about this time my mother was asked to allow me to take part in a *tableau vivant* with some other small children: we were to sit absolutely still, I with a doll in my lap in costume. We had a gauze screen to make it look like a picture. Mother was willing but I wasn't and flatly refused to take part so nothing could be done about it.

Then came the Boer War in 1899–1901 and the death of Victoria. We had left Rosemount Place in May 1898 to live at Northfield, a new semi-detached house overlooking the North Inch. I remember coming home from a violin lesson and bearing the news of the Relief of Mafeking to my parents who had not heard about it – no radio in those days – and I returned before the evening paper arrived. My father, who was in the garden, carried me shoulder high up the garden to the house to tell my mother. Baden-Powell was the hero of that day, later to achieve popularity as the founder of the Scout Movement, which leads me on a few years to 1906 when I was at school in Scarborough. Some of us were taken to a lecture given on scouting with slides by BP himself. As in those days one always dressed up for any evening occasion, we were in school evening outfit of white dresses with scarlet hooded cloaks; Baden-Powell in his concluding words said it had almost seemed like a wedding with such an array of bridesmaids facing him. It pays to dress up. Nowadays we would only have been wearing daytime uniform.

My next decade was Edwardian. Father and Mother used to bicycle a great deal and go for picnics in company with a crowd of their friends. Other hobbies of Father's were golf, fishing and curling in season. They cycled to many places around Perth, and the Sma' Glen was a favourite ride.

At the time Edward VII was to have been crowned I went with my parents to stay with a bachelor friend of my father who owned an attractive Border tower at Melrose, Dornick Tower, in June of 1902. The house with adjoining hall-house had crow-stepped gables and these were to have been lit by 'fairy-lights' – these were coloured glass jars or vases about three-quarters of an inch high with a night light in each, one to be put on each step, each a different colour, outlining the building with jewels. But alas, Edward fell ill with appendicitis but his surgeon operated successfully. In those days an appendix removal was considered a very serious operation, surgery having made very little progress. Knowledge which came later through the 1914–18 war was learned the hard way. So the coronation had to be postponed and we never had our display, greatly to my disappointment. The tower was the most intriguing place to stay. In the tower portion there was a spiral staircase with right-handed turn to leave the sword-arm free play and lit by arrow-slot windows. I had a little bedroom in the tower itself, all panelled in dark wood with a bed built across the end of it. There was a speaking-tube by which we could communicate with the ground floor; the hall and other rooms above ground level were in a later part of the building, with the kitchen at ground level. There were some quite spacious grounds with fine lawns and trees and some flowerbeds. Apart from the tower was the old Dower House which at the time was standing empty. We were shown the entrance to a priest's hole which was quite far up in one of the cavernous chimneys.

Bicycle and charabanc parties were summer entertainments, whist or bridge in winter, with soirées, evening parties and tea parties for the ladies. Tennis became very popular and Nigger minstrel and Banjo bands were all the rage – the banjos decorated with pink ribbons and sashes.

When we lived at Northfield on the North Inch, the Perth Hunt steeplechase races ran past our windows so there were three days of excitement each September, added to which there were all sorts of society people staying at Balhousie Castle not so far from us where the Earl of Kinnoull entertained for the week. He was a gay bachelor and always looked very distinguished in a kilt of the Hay tartan. I think he had a pretty choice of lady friends of whom my parents must have disapproved as I was never allowed to go to the Race Balls although all my friends did. The other local 'laird' was Lord Mansfield of Scone Palace where later the Races were held in the Palace Park.

I suppose the next major event was 'coming out'. Girls on leaving school did not immediately get jobs, in fact for us it was an entirely social life, though some perhaps carried out social service work. One was not accepted into adult society fully until one had made one's debut at a Public Dance. In the winter of 1908–09 I 'put my hair up' and 'came out' at a ball given by the Royal Golf Club of which my father was a member. The Club had not given such an entertainment ever before but it was very well run with Joyce's Band which was 'the' dance band of the day, and a sumptuous sit-down supper with wonderful food to eat and champagne to drink, all for only a guinea a head. The Bachelors also gave a dance the same winter – this took place in the Station Hotel and was by invitation only. Several smaller dances made up my first season.

At a public dance girls always had to have chaperones. If the girl's mother could not attend there was always some old hen who would mother a number of chickens; girls had to remain near mother or chaperone between dances or if not dancing any number. They could attend a private dance unchaperoned as the hostess stood in lieu. There were always programmes and the first dance was nearly always taken by booking up if you were a man or being booked up if you were a girl, and most important it was to have a full card so as not to lose face. On the other hand one was looked at askance if one booked more than two dances with one particular man, and his attentions were questioned if this were done. Of course, the supper dance was with one's particular friend. If you had booked up a full programme and someone arrived late with whom you would have liked to have danced, well that was just too bad; you must on no account cut someone's dance to fit in the preferred partner.

When I first came out there were only the Waltzes, Polka, Schottisches, Reels, Lancers, Pas de Quatre, Washington Post (a similar dance to the Pas de Quatre), on the programme which always finished with the Post Horn Gallop. Gradually the Foxtrot, Two-step and One-step came in and a slow form of the Waltz, the Boston, and an early form of Tango up to the time of the 1914–18 war.

At these balls there was always a huge sit-down supper and devilled bones or poached eggs at 4 a.m.. Balls lasted from 9 p.m. to 4 a.m. and dances from 9 p.m. to 2 a.m. At private dances there was always a jolly good supper as well and one had a good rest and was ready for the second half of the evening's entertainment. At all balls and dances, sitting-out places (two seats only, together) were provided, so if you didn't want to dance or only part of any dance you could find some selected corner to chat or flirt with your partner. I imagine that with a few there were quite some goings-on in these spots but as a rule I expect it was only the shy kiss that was given.

No make-up was ever worn by nice girls, not even a dust of powder – only actresses and rather go-ahead society women ever made-up. I only began to use a little powder myself about 1923, encouraged to do so after a visit to Monsieur Henri, the hairdresser in Penrith, who remarked to me, looking at my reflection in the mirror as he was doing my hair, 'A leetle powdaire would soften zee face!'

In the years after I came out I had a pleasant social life with dances and tennis parties, and mixed foursomes at golf. Father used to take me to dances, Mother preferred to stay at home and, low be it spoken, I enjoyed myself more in her absence, although I had always to account to her with whom I had danced and tell what all the other girls were wearing etc etc next day. The big Edinburgh balls I went to and similar ones in Perth in the Assembly Rooms and County Buildings were very gay, colourful and enjoyable with tip-top bands, fortune Viennese and sometimes with pipers for the reels and strathspeys. In the Assembly Rooms and Music Room there was always a special décor in Egyptian style or some other theatrical scenery stagesetting. Suppers were excellent with champagne or wine or soft drinks – usually cold consommé, turkey, ham, salads, sweets, ice pudding, fruit and coffee and before leaving at about 3 a.m. hot soup and devilled bones.

Cricket matches of which my paternal grandfather was a great supporter were also played every summer on the Inch. Once a cricketing friend going out to bat forgot to take out his glass eye in the dressing-room, so he presented it on his way out to my grandfather for safekeeping during his innings.

In 1907 my father took me one weekend to Pitlochry Hydro. He used also to take me out early before breakfast and sometimes after tea to coach me in the Royal and Ancient game in which I became fairly proficient with a handicap of 12 (Ladies Golf Union). Later he did the same with tennis. Mother played a little gentle golf with me but never played tennis although before marriage she had played in Edinburgh. Looking back, I wonder why I never questioned why. She was an accomplished skater, figure skater and dancer. But she never enjoyed the freedom of movement that I have had – women did not go to public functions without their husbands, though men would go without their wives.

She would give word to the maids to say she was not 'At Home' to casual callers; she only liked visitors who came on her 'At Home' day once a month or who were specially invited. Often visitors called next day after the 'At Home' day was over, but – no admission, Mother would not be taken unawares. When we were alone, we had for tea only bread and butter or toast and the tea in the brown earthenware pot, and such fare could not be offered to visitors, so the silver pot, sugar basin, cream jug etc were all only taken out of their chamois leather bags on 'At Home' days. Elegant sandwiches, scones, cakes and biscuits were prepared and a lace tablecloth put out, and the drawing-room fire lit before lunch so that the room would be warm, which of course it never was until late in the evening. As visitors kept their outdoor coats and hats on, it is to be hoped they did not feel so cold. Some visitors were carriage folk and only stayed a brief time while the coachman drove his landau with one or two horses up and down or round the block at walking pace so that the horses did not take cold.

Calls on 'At Home' days were for the purpose mostly of returning thanks after being invited previously to lunch or dinner or to a private dance. The etiquette of calling was very strict. A lady when visiting a married couple (and married herself), if she found her hostess at home, left two of her husband's cards on a tray in the hall left specially for the purpose. The corner of one of these was turned up which meant she had called in person. If there was no one at home, the lady left her own card as well. If she had daughters 'out', i.e. having left school 'finished', their names were inscribed below Mama's name, the eldest girl as Miss, the others as Miss Jane, Miss Sarah etc. This was still in force when I was of an age to be on Mother's calling cards in 1906. People leaving a district always paid a last call and left cards even if the hostess was at home, with PPC written in one corner – 'pour prendre congé' [to take leave]. Single ladies had their own cards also but of course left only one for the lady of the house. Brides had to wait until they were first called upon, then round they had to go in turn to all who had condescended to call upon them. Well, they had little to do, so I suppose this all helped to pass the time. In the case of death, one used black-edged cards both for calling and being called upon; edges were a quarter-inch black for the first six months, then half that width for the next six months and for the third six months quite a thin edge. The same applied to notepaper which often was not white but what was called 'silurian' grey. Gradually these distinctions were dropped but even up to World War One a thin black edge was used for a time.

Father and Mother used to go to concerts to which I was taken at an early age – about 5 or 6 – and to performances of the Gilbert and Sullivan operas given by the D' Oyley Carte Opera Company. I usually wore a smoked cream cashmere dress and had a Red Riding Hood evening cape in pink grosgrain lined with white, black openwork stockings and patent leather shoes with ankle straps. At these concerts I first saw my Aunt Caroline, Father's sister, and two friends, Mary Pullar and Claire Fleming, playing the violin, which fired me with the ambition to do likewise – I was not drawn to the banjo or mandolin as so many others were. Some years later I heard Lady Halle (Norma Nemda) at a big concert – she was one of the few lady violinists of the period and I well remember the thrill this gave me as by this time I was learning to play myself.

I first saw cinema in 1896 at a private house and I saw a similar early machine at an exhibition in 1956.

Life continued in this carefree way until in 1910 Edward VII died. 1911 brought the coronation of George V when we had a grand pageant and many other celebrations. The pageant consisted of decorated horse-drawn lorries; first, one with Britannia, then England, Scotland, Ireland, Wales and one each also for the different colonies of the British Empire. I was on the Scottish car as one of the 'four Marys' attending Mary Stuart, with Queen Mary seated on a throne and the four girls posed around. I was glad to have the chair back to hold onto. This cavalcade drove all round town, rattling over streets that were still cobbled, and our leg muscles vibrated hugely; we finally ended up on the North Inch all drawn up in orderly array, where we were inspected and judged by some VIP or other and prizes were awarded accordingly. At night there was a dance and supper in the Royal George Hotel at which we still wore our costumes. My daughters also wore this dress (for dressing-up) thirty years later, and this year in 1971 I am wearing nightdresses trimmed with the lace which I saved from the ruff and veil worn some fifty years ago which cost 3d per yard.

A few more years of this sort of life and then trouble and World War One broke out in 1914. Things were never the same. Girls were allowed a great deal more freedom to do things on their own. I went off in 1916 to work in a Remount Depot at Worcester, helping to make surgical dressings (from sphagnum moss) and hospital garments and knitting. Then in 1917 I got married.

7

Friends and Etiquette

Where are my friends? – I am alone,
No playmate shares my beaker.
Some lie beneath the churchyard stone
And some before the Speaker;
And some compose a tragedy,
And some compose a rondo;
And some draw swords for liberty,
And some draw pleas for John Doe.
(Praed, 'School and Schoolfellows')

WHEN I look back to my youth and count the number of real friends my parents and I had, it seems quite amazing when now they barely total the fingers of one hand – acquaintances are the more numerous.

Of course, life was so very different before the 1914 war brought such tremendous changes to everything. Before this, people travelled much less and did not leave home except for the annual holiday with all the family.

One got to know everyone very well as people were born, lived, married and died in the same place. Young people married others from local families and in their particular social circle – and these circles were very strictly observed. There were several social 'grades'. First, the County, as they were called – those with large estates and possibly titles, who were always very pleasant and agreeable if and when one met them on public and formal occasions, like the Kinnoulls and Mansfields. My father had most contact with these people as he met them at his club, the Royal Perth Golfing Society, and on business occasions. Next in the pecking order came the people who had smaller estates and fair-sized country houses, kept a carriage and horses and retained a good staff of servants. Some of these people were very pleasant but others rather put on airs and were a bit 'toffee-nosed' and so were dubbed by my father as 'the cod-fish County'.

We met our friends at dances, theatres, concerts and at sports. There were a few public balls but mostly small private dances given by those who had rooms large enough and by others at an hotel. Some houses had fine parquet floors but often the carpet was covered by 'drugget' – this was coarse woven damask sheet which was stretched very, very tightly so that it could not ruck up while we danced. It was quite slippery and a powder was sprinkled over it to help.

One of our family's best friends was Corrie Chisholm – a horsy, doggy, gardening lady, a great sport for tennis, bicycling and picnicking and very kind to me as a child. She had a marvellous maid called Swan who had a cat called Doolie. Corrie and Mother and I, when I was old enough, went for days in the country on foot or bicycle to places like Glenfarg. She was a great photographer too. I well remember the ham and egg teas, with treacle and drop scones we came back to at her house, Barn Hill, close to the railway – at one short-cut approach we had to walk along the track and I was always fearful lest a train come along while we were so doing although there was not the slightest danger if one did. Swan and Doolie had to be visited after tea and the large white deal table with the furry leg noted – Doolie's scratching post.

Corrie rode and drove a smart dogcart outfit, was keen on dogs, a masculine type with a wicked gleam of mischief in her eye. Philip and Diana both had tea with her when they were little. She died after we were in Kenya.

Our particular friends were among the professional people, i.e. lawyers, clergy, artists, writers and some who had big businesses such as the Pullars, Moncrieffs and Gloags. Tradespeople and shopkeepers were only in the acquaintance grade and accepted socially when they prospered and became better off. One's doctor was never on the social visiting list until about 1912 – snobbery was appalling before then. The smaller-fry tradespeople were quite apart from the rest and had their own strata of society and friends.

The Pullar family began in a very humble way; they started the famous dyeing and cleaning business, the husband and wife going round with a handcart to the various houses collecting soiled clothes for washing. This was done in an artificial stream which ran through Perth and linked up the Almond and Tay rivers. In those days, this stream, or lade, as it was called, was 'open' but was later covered over. I can remember when part of it was still open and ran along the town side of the North Inch. The business prospered and developed; later generations started the dyeing sections – which progressed well when James Pullar (of my grandfather's generation) married a German wife, Adelgunde by name, and thereby learned all about aniline dyes from the Germans, which were more permanent than the old vegetable dyes. Both Lady Pullar and rather formidable Adelgunde were replicas of Queen Victoria in style and dress and grand manner.

James Pullar had a large house and grounds in the same district in Perth as the Grey family – Bowerswell. He had a son Herbert and a daughter Mary. As far as I can remember, she died at an early age; Herbert married a very nice lady, Rhoda, who died at over ninety in 1968. They lived at Bridge of Earn, had no family but were very hospitable, giving tennis parties and every winter a most excellent dance in their own home with a tip-top supper laid on by a caterer and a good three-piece band. Here it was I first sampled the delicacy Pêche Melba which was produced by a famous chef in honour of the singer Nellie Melba.

James's elder brother Sir Robert Pullar lived in Tayside in a large house on the riverfront and was knighted for services to citizenship. He had two sons, Albert and Rufus, who were both married with families just a little younger than I was. The Alberts lived in another house on the riverfront while Rufus built himself a house a mile out of Perth at Hillyland where the dyeworks had a large factory.

Albert had four daughters, Helen, Dorothy, Christian and Marjorie. Rufus had two sons, Maurice, who sadly was a hunchback, and Lindsay, a good-looking boy but rather conceited and not nearly as nice as his unfortunate brother. I was frequently a guest at parties in winter and to 'tea' on other occasions and later on to play tennis. All the Pullars were very hospitable and every year there were good parties for young people to which I was invited.

Mother and the Pullar ladies were on calling terms; they visited each other on special 'At Home' days but it was all very formal. After I had left school old Lady Pullar died and a widowed niece of Sir Robert's came to keep house for him. She had a daughter of my age, Norah Keyworth, and I met her at some Pullar house and then was invited to Tayside. We used to play billiards after tea – in the billiards room there were two white marble busts of Sir Robert and his lady draped in white muslin to keep them free of dust.

My first introduction to the violin was hearing Mary Pullar playing a solo at a concert given in Perth City Hall; she played on her mother's Guarnerius violin – I must have been about six. Later I was taken to hear Norma Neruda (Lady Halle) play a concerto and was thrilled by the performance. When it was coming up to my seventh birthday my grandfather Thomas asked what I would like for Christmas and my birthday – he usually gave me one present for both dates. I asked for a violin and was given a beginner's outfit, costing in those days a pound, for a half-size violin, bow and green felt-lined wooden case with a piece of rosin thrown in. I may say that the violin was of much better quality than the terrible crude Chinese instruments made today for the beginner. I started to have lessons in April 1898.

One member of the St Johnston's Orchestra was my friend Charles Sillar who played the cello. One day when I was with my father in town, Charles was going along the opposite side of the street, cello under arm; father crossed and, without saying a word, pressed a penny into Charles's hand and passed on. Charles stopped, looked at the penny, laughed and put it in his pocket. In the orchestra, 'nice lady my auntie' Caroline led. Claire Fleming, daughter of Dr Fleming, Minister of St Paul's Church at the top of the High Street, was another violinist and was one of the fortunates to be lent Adelgunde's Guarnerius. She it was when taken to Forfar to supplement the local players in a performance of Dvorak's 'Spectre's Bride', who arrived late with her partner, a young man at the first desk. After Herr Feurberg had been unable to wait for them any longer and was about to tap his desk for us to start, they came hurriedly onto the platform. Herr Feurberg looked daggers at them and said 'Joost scanalous!' Claire's brother Archibald was also a clergyman and became Head of the Church of Scotland in London. I first played chamber music at the house of Provost Smythe of St Ninian's Cathedral – Mrs Smythe played viola and was also a member of the orchestra. Mrs McCall Smith was another cellist who was very friendly to me.

Norah Urquhart was the youngest daughter of a Dr Urquhart who was in charge of a large private asylum. We gave entertainments periodically for the patients and an annual Fancy Dress Ball was held. When I went to play for the patients my accompanist was one of the patients who was a very good pianist. He was well enough to go out in his own horse and trap, and one of the young student doctors was told one day to take Mr Petter out and see he came to no harm; unfortunately he lost him until he heard shouts coming from nearby bushes and a voice saying, 'Don't tell Dr Agassiz I am here.' This young doctor asked cousin Maisie and me if we would like to come to Blairgowrie for the day and play a mixed foursome at golf and have lunch at the hotel with Mr Petter – we were to go there in Mr Petter's chauffeur driven car. Strange to say, my usually fearful mother allowed us to go and we had a nice day – Mr Petter partnering me at golf as I knew him quite well from musical visits. Dr Young told us that when we got to the hotel, the manager said, 'So you have some lady patients with you today', to which the doctor said he answered, 'Oh yes, but they are quite well behaved and harmless'. He was always full of fun. Another of the young medicos there died of diabetes, which was very sad; today he would have lived.

A great link with the past for me was knowing some of the Gray family who lived at Bowerswell near to the James Pullars. Effie Gray (Euphemia) was first married to John Ruskin; he refused to consummate the marriage so she brought a nullity suit in 1854 and in 1855 married Millais the painter. The picture by Millais of 'Bubbles' which Pears used as their famous advertisement was of Admiral Sir William James, Effie's grandson, as a child. I remember Effie Gray's younger brother Melville, who lived at Bowerswell House until he died in 1945 aged 98. He never married, was very hospitable, gave frequent tennis and clock golf parties for young people, was very interested in racing and kept a complete list of all the Derby winners in his Bible.

Effie Gray's mother was a Sophie Jameson. The Jamesons were a well-known Perth family in legal business – the following two generations being friends

of my parents and myself. Harry Gray was a great friend
of my father and Mrs of Mother, but for all that they
knew each other so well they never called each other
by their Christian names – it was always Mrs Harry and
Mrs John.

Three brothers called James, George and Jack
Miller were friends of my father. James must have
been somewhat older as I cannot remember what his
business was; I can only recollect him as a golfer and
fisherman. I once found a cast he had accidentally left
on the bank of the Tay near the North Inch – Father
guessed whose it must be and returned it to James who
kindly had it made into a salmon fly brooch for me – I
still have it. George was tall and thin, in legal business,
with an everlasting cigarette. He bred Shetland ponies
which were delightful, about the size of a huge Airedale
terrier, dark chestnut with creamy crimped manes and
tails and very frisky; he used to drive a four-in-hand
with a light landau-type carriage and win prizes for
turnout at the local shows.

He had a prim little wife Margaret, who was very
interested in prison welfare work; she conducted a
sewing class in Perth prison every week and frequently
used to take me along to play my violin to the women
when I was a child. In the intervals she read to them
and I played two or three selections of Scotch airs
and simple tunes. She was overheard one day saying
to someone, 'You know I've been to prison for forty
years', greatly to the astonishment of others nearby

who were not quite sure what she meant. Another of her sayings was that one must always be sure one's underclothes were clean because one never knew but one might have an accident and it would be dreadful to be found wearing soiled linen. I well remember the opening of the huge studded door to the prison and the reception at the office before a wardress took us across the yard into the prison, up iron staircases all open work, and along gallery passages to the room where the class was held, bare of everything but a few raised benches and tables and an iron stove. There was a raised dais at one end where the piano was and a table and chairs for Mrs Miller and me. She went round the class of two dozen women and supervised their work, sewing and knitting. The women were dressed in gowns, very shapeless, of some coarse grey material with broad arrows here and there, an apron and a sort of mob cap, and soft string-soled slippers to make sure they had no handy weapon such as a leather shoe heel. George and Margaret Miller had one daughter, Kitty, who was long and lank and awkward of movement. She distinguished herself one day at dancing by doing the sword dance in reverse, widder-shins: the dancing master, smiling, said: 'Well I couldn't do that!'

Mrs Miller had a sister who was a bit odd. In winter she lived with her sister and brother-in-law at Knowehead but in the summer months she went to live outside Perth where the Millers had a small place where George kept his ponies. I remember Mother saying to a cook we had then at Gaskhill, on the opposite side of the road from Knowehead, 'I haven't seen Miss Wallace for some time.' 'Oh!' replied Jessie, 'She's bin pit awa for the summer!'

Other families who made money in trade were the Lumsdens, who had bleaching fields and linen works at Huntingtower, and the Mackenzies who were also in legal business. The Lumsdens had a nice place near Huntingtower and gave tennis parties in summer and dances in winter; James and his wife were contemporary with my parents and their family Effie, Laura, David, Molly and Grizel were my friends. As regards the Mackenzies, George was in the firm of Condie Mackenzie & Co, and had by his first wife Jennie, David and Emily, slightly older than myself, and then later he married his housekeeper and had a second family. They lived in Atholl Crescent at the foot of Charlotte Street next to Blackfriars School. Also in Atholl Crescent lived Dr James Stirling with a large family; the youngest James is now a judge. Our own doctor, who lived in Charlotte Street, was Dr Ferguson with one daughter Muffie who went to Blackfriars School – otherwise unknown to me. After Dr Ferguson died, we had a Dr Taylor and by that time things had become less formal and we were able to call on his wife and meet for bridge and tea parties. The Buist family also lived in Atholl Crescent and were three girls and three boys; the youngest David died of lockjaw [tetanus] through getting his hand cut on a piece of bracken. I can remember the shock quite plainly when we heard of his death. There were no anti-tetanus injections in those days.

To another social stratum belonged the families called Noad, tea merchants, and Moncreiff who had glass and ink factories and were considered as tradesmen and only to be acknowledged as such until industry and improvement in their financial circumstances enabled them to come to the fore. They were then in far better financial circumstances and bought large homes along the riverside which the professional classes could not afford to do, so they were on the same plane as the Pullars and welcomed in society for all entertainments. A Moncreiff sister married a Noad and had a son Jock who used to wear Little Lord Faunterloy-type clothes for best and had long ringlets. They lived in Rosemount Place and Jock used to ride what he called his 'trisillick' horse up and down, greatly to my envy as I was not allowed to play with him – they not being considered in the same class of society as we were. Time, however, was to prove different; as the years passed they became more affluent and lived in much better houses than we did. Later still I was to meet Jock in Kenya where he was a PWD [Public Works Department] official married to his cousin Hope and they had one little girl – then I lost track again.

When we lived at Northfield opposite the North Inch we were not far from Balhousie Castle which was owned by the then Lord Kinnoull and I presume was let to a family called Alison – Mr Alison, his daughter Effie, ages with me, and his two sisters. I used to go often and play with her and they gave delightful parties at Hallowe'en and in the Christmas hols. She was a large awkward girl but good-natured, with a large mop of fiery red hair.

Father had business with the whisky family Dewar, who lived at Dupplin Castle, once belonging to the Hay family, Earls of Kinnoull; otherwise we did not meet except at Christmas parties. Once when I was about twelve I played at a pupils' concert in a trio for three violins with two of the Dewar girls who were also being taught by Gottlieb Feurberg; both were much taller than I was so I was given Part 2 to play – 'We cannot have ziz ladder business,' said Gottlieb. At parties one met Dewar sons (of another brother), one of whom was later to become the very well-known racehorse owner and winner of classic races. He was a very good-looking, nice boy and I was greatly smitten but as our meetings were only once or twice a year at parties our acquaintance remained just that. I met 'my fate' (as it was known in those days) at the United Services Club Ball in Edinburgh in 1912.

I lost touch with my earliest and most intimate friend, Edith (Tootee) Leslie after Christmas 1965. I last saw her at Tynefield when Susan was two or three years old and we corresponded every Christmas until 1965 but next year no answering letter came to mine.

8

Prices and Housekeeping

L IVING was very simple in our household when I was a child. My mother received £10 per month for housekeeping up to 1900. This covered meat, groceries, vegetables and fruit, fish, milk, laundry – including the washerwoman at 2/6, firewood and small sundries for my parents, myself and two maids. Fuel, lighting bills, wines and whisky (at 3/6 a bottle) were paid by Father.

Beef was 9d to 1/- per lb, mutton 6d to 1/- per lb, ham a luxury, rabbits 6d to 10d each, boiling fowl 2/6 each, young chickens 5/- to 6/- each, a goose 8d per lb, a turkey 1/- per lb.

Bread was 4d to 6d a 2-lb loaf, milk was 1d per pint poured into a jug by the roundsman from his churn, butter was 1/- per lb, fresh butter 1/6 per lb, sugar 2d per lb, tea from 6d upwards per ¼ lb, a ¼ lb of coffee 1/-, a soda siphon 1/-, bottles 4d, splits 2d. Matches were ½d per box, cigarettes 5 for 2½d, pipe tobacco

6d per oz. Jam was 8d for 2 lb, marmalade 10d for 2 lb. Eggs were 10d to 1/- per dozen.

Fish was 6d per lb for cod, herrings 1d each and a pair of kippers 4d. At the greengrocer's, cucumbers, peas, beans and cauliflowers were considered a luxury, as was most fruit and seldom bought except for a pound of eating apples at the weekend. A melon was 6d, oranges 1d to 4d each and those were seasonal at Christmas. We bought carrots, turnips and occasionally cabbage; potatoes were ½d to 1d per lb, new potatoes 6d to 8d per lb. Bananas were hung up in big green bunches at the greengrocer's and sold at ½d each. An iced sponge cake was 6d, a fruitcake was 1/-. Sweets were cheap with 8 chocolate gingers for 1d, 'Parleys', a type of ginger biscuit, for ½d each and Bath buns for 1d.

Coal was 14/- a ton, and sticks were 1/- a bag (sack). Peats in the west of Scotland at 3/6 a bag were considered expensive. Rail fares were 1d per mile, and 1½d return per mile. Cab fare was 1/- to 1/6 per mile.

Plain single sheets were 10/- each, cotton material 1/- per yard. Children's shoes were 2/6 and 5/- per pair, ladies' were 5/- to £1 1/- and men's 10/- upwards. Shoe repairs cost about 2/6 to 4/- for soling and heeling, perhaps 5/6 for men's shoes.

Books and novels were 2/6 to 5/-; the cheap edition of Cassell's Classics were 6d although bound, hardbacked of course. In 1897, magazines were *The*

Strand, Pearson's Royal Novel and *Windsor* at 1/- each;
Answers 2d, *Titbits* 2d, *Pearson's Weekly* 2d, *Punch* 3d, *The
Graphic* 6d, and *Scots Pictorial* 3d. Pencils, best quality,
1d each. Letterpost was 1d, for postcards ½d. Telegrams
cost 6d for 12 words, ½d for each additional word.
Before 1914, there were only £5 notes in paper money
– large white ones, then £1 and 10/- notes came in.

The theatre in Perth cost 3/6 in the Dress Circle.
There were many little toys for 1d each. 'Books for
Bairns' sold at 1d each, titles such as *Brer Rabbit*.
'Nankeen' dolls were ½d, Dutch dolls 6d and 1/-.
Cardboard cut-out toy theatres were popular for
children.

Our food was very basic compared with what people
expect today. For breakfast Father had porridge, fish
or eggs, or sausage – never bacon – baps and tea; the
maids had porridge, bread and butter. For the midday
meal, Father had sandwiches or lunch at the Club;
Mother had milk and bread and butter, the maids and
I had meat and potatoes – never a green vegetable –
and plain boiled milk pudding.

Meat was stewed steak, Irish stew, mince or rabbit.
Vegetables were usually carrot or turnip – peas, beans
or cauliflower were only for lunches given to visitors.
Only cooked fruit – prunes, apples and rhubarb – was
eaten except on very special occasions. A roast was
cooked for Saturday night late dinner and used cold
on Sunday and as hash on Monday. Tea for everybody
was bread and butter. A 6d gingerbread or sandwich

cake was bought for Sunday tea, cakes were very seldom made at home and, if so, were gingerbreads and plain white cakes. Pastry and steamed puddings were hardly ever made, but soup was.

Father and Mother had a two-course dinner at 7.30 p.m. which was very plain. I joined them at the age of fourteen and then I had the milk and bread and butter lunch. Before this, my evening meal had been porridge, bread and butter. I never had jam; rhubarb was the only kind ever made at home and marmalade was never made, nor was fruit bottled. Very little fruit was bought – strawberries perhaps once a year. Father used to bring home 2 lb of apples at the weekend in the winter and a melon in the summer, and I was given sparingly of both. Ice cream was a luxury indulged in twice in the summer at the most. Mother and I would meet Father in town and he took us to a confectioner's shop where we went to a very dark room at the back with dark-green marble-topped tables and bentwood chairs and ate our ices off glass plates. I used to spend my Saturday penny at this shop and could get eight chocolate gingers for that sum. The ices cost 4d and were larger than the 9d ones of today and were real cream ices, no mixtures.

The only times when food was more luxurious were the teas on Mother's monthly 'At Home' days and when they gave luncheon and dinner parties. I often used to wonder when I was older if visitors thought these meals were typical of our everyday fare or if all other families lived in this way. Mother would never be taken completely unawares, but never kept a supply of stores, so that a special meal could be prepared for a chance visitor. It was all very formal.

The housemaid set the table, carried in the food and waited at table. Soup was served at table from a large tureen with a big ladle. Meat was carved at the main table, vegetables were handed by the maid who often remained standing by the door of the room while her employers ate their meal, ready to anticipate their wants. There were always white damask tablecloths and table napkins, butter in small pats or curls, and the salt in the saltcellars moulded into a neat round with an eggcup or pressed flat and patterned with the saltspoon.

Part Two:
Diana Brisco Malik
(née Rimington)

Part Two
Diana Krista Malik
(née Kinnington)

9

Continuing the History

IN THE interest of continuing history, I feel an urge to add to my mother's descriptions of her life during her childhood from 1890 to 1910.

My English grandfather, George Arthur Rimington, County Magistrate, lived at Tynefield, Penrith. I remember him as a large austere old gentleman with a big moustache who perhaps only once took me on his knee. He attended the County Sessions in Carlisle as a County Judge and he liked hunting and shooting.

My English grandmother, Frances Dykes Brisco, was first cousin to my grandfather. Their first child, a daughter called Janet, was born out of wedlock and taken to France where she was fostered. This was done because it was such a disgrace to have an illegitimate child in those days – to have a child from the wrong side of the bedclothes, so to speak. Janet grew up in France and had a daughter, Alice, who married a man much older than herself called Auguste. All this was very 'hush-hush' in the family, never spoken about – the family skeleton in the cupboard. But, Alice was proud that she had English forebears and used to correspond regularly with my mother whom she liked and quite often she would come to England on holiday and visit my mother and they would talk to each other in French. After the war, Alice came on a visit to England, and as I was studying in London, I was able to accompany her on some sightseeing trips. I also went across to France and stayed with her for about a week, and she took me about and showed me the French way of life, visiting the open markets, and she even took me to the Folies Bergères.

My grandfather had two maiden sisters called Great Aunt Florrie and Great Aunt Annie. They both lived in a huge house in Lowther Street. I seem to remember seeing them once only when I was very small. According to my mother they were typical Edwardian ladies, very prim and proper, who spent their days trying to decide how to trim their corsage or their hats. One would say to the other, 'Annie, do you think this little bit of lace looks alright here?' and Annie would reply, 'Not really, my dear Florrie. Try that velvet ribbon instead.' They never threw any letters away and on their death my mother and father had to sort through all the letters – trunks and trunks of them.

My grandfather had a relatively famous brother, General Michael Rimington, who founded 'The Rimington Scouts' who fought in the Boer War and who had their own distinctive uniform and hat. He was a very harsh general and there are cruel stories of how he punished his young officers, which I would not like to describe.

My English grandparents had eight children, Janet, Ethel, Michael, Camilla, Evie, Alice, George and Geoffrey (my father). Janet I met only once in her maisonette in Paris, which had a very grim black interior. She could speak French only and was very dour. Her daughter Alice was typically French and quite extravert. Ethel was a flabby fat lady who was once Mayor of Carlisle. She had two children, Nancy and a son Hugh who was injured in a motor-cycle crash. Aunt Ethel was one of my godparents, but I never even got a tuppenny ha'penny sweet from her. Michael I cannot remember at all. George, or Lester as he was most often called, married an American woman, Sheila, and the two of them descended on us once at Tynefield in the 1930s in their flashy convertible Studebaker car, she with her fox-fur stole and 'pooch' dog tucked under her arm. She seemed to be an adored but very spoilt wife. They never had children. Alice married Hartley Graham, a descendant of Fletcher Christian of 'The Mutiny on the Bounty'. Fletcher Christian came from the Workington area, I believe. Hartley Graham was a revered solicitor in Bishop Yards in Penrith and they lived in a huge house called The Larches (which is now an hotel). We used to be taken there for tea, and I used to be in awe of the huge house with its very long corridors. They also had a grass tennis court, a large walled vegetable garden and two very big greenhouses, smelling deliciously of hot vines and peach trees. They had four children. Young Hartley was an Oxford 'grad' who was killed at Dunkirk in a slit trench. I imagined old Hartley never recovered from the shock as he died soon after. I was very saddened as he was my godfather and I loved him dearly as he had always had patience for me.

Michael, the second son, had been to Cambridge and was a Cambridge Blue. I can remember seeing his oars displayed on the wall in the hallway of The Larches. Michael worked in the same office as his father, but became rather odd in his later life. There was some instability in his make-up as there definitely was in his mother who was very odd. However, she did play in one of the early Wimbledon Championships and painted beautiful watercolours. Bridget was the eldest daughter. She trained as a Norland Nanny and after various jobs she changed to Roman Catholicism in order to take a job in France. When that job came to an end, she converted back again and married 'Steve' – a regular Cavalry officer. They had two children one of whom was born with cerebral palsy and had to be put in a children's home. Rosemary, the youngest of Hartley Graham's family, trained as a PE teacher but soon after met and married a dashing RAF officer. I remember a big party was thrown at The Larches at the christening of her firstborn.

Aunt Evie was big and bossy but quite friendly. She was married to Arthur Wilkinson – an estate manager to Lord Iliffe in Yattendon. They had two children: Henry who was killed at the age of eighteen in a motor-cycle crash and Molly who married Squadron Leader Wallace-Kyle, an Australian; they had four children. He became Sir Wallace-Kyle and Governor of Western Australia. Aunt Camilla married Neville Smith and they lived near Yattendon. She played tennis, but he did not. I thought he was a very 'dull' man. They had no children. My Scottish grandfather was Honorary Sheriff-Substitute for Perth, having been a colonel in the Black Watch Regiment. My Scottish grandmother was a sweet old lady but according to my mother she did absolutely nothing but sit behind closed blinds doing the *Scotsman* crossword puzzle and reading. My mother was their only child whom they encouraged in her music, but because of World War One they would not let her go to Germany for further study. It was her one big regret that she never had advanced teaching. However, she availed herself of it later on in life when she had enough money.

Our Scottish grandparents were very good to us – more so than our English grandparents. Grandfather and Grandmother Thomas bought us innumerable toys and books and sent out toys and goodies every Christmas when we were in Kenya.

Of the other members of the Scottish family, I did meet, but only once, Aunt Susie Wyse (sister of my grannie) and Aunt Carrie (sister of my grandfather). I also got to know Mother's cousin Maisie who was well off but a bit of a snob. However, she was quite kind to me when I was studying in London.

Geoffrey, my father, the youngest, was told quite bluntly by his father to go out and find his own way in the world. So he went to the outbacks of Canada, Kamloops in fact, doing I know not what, but later he joined the British Columbia Police and became smitten with riding. He returned after some years and met my mother at a ball in Edinburgh and swept her off her feet. They were quite go-ahead because she told me that he used to ride a motor-cycle with her in the side-car. He drove all the way from Edinburgh to Penrith – about 300 miles – in one day. My father served in World War One, reaching the rank of captain and winning the Military Cross. But that is another story.

10

Early Years

FATHER and Mother married in 1917 and I was born in 1922. My early years were for the most part spent in Kenya where my father was a district commissioner appointed by the Crown Agents. In England, one of my first memories, strangely enough like my mother's, was seeing the lamplighter lighting the gas street lamps with a hook on a long pole. We were living in a house in Wordsworth Street, Penrith, probably as part of an extended leave from Kenya, because my father had six months' 'home-leave' every two and a half years from his tour in Kenya. Compared to my mother's rather sheltered way of life in her early days, the era of my childhood was definitely advancing due to the development of transport and communications.

Although we encountered some appalling roads in the Kenya Highlands, great areas were now being opened up for the combustion engine. Radio, for us at least, was still only the 'crystal set' type and I cannot remember any other far-reaching telecommunications system, but mail and provisions did reach us at fairly regular intervals at our far outpost in the colony.

Life was still very simple, but one had either to get used to, or alternatively, not get used to, the colonial way of life. My father absolutely revelled in it – tennis, drinks, Bridge, safaris, the lot! On the other hand, my mother simply detested it – the artificiality of it. She longed for a bit of culture and was not very happy in the role of being a memsahib.

Although I was just four, I can vaguely remember the wooden bungalow and life in Kisumu. My brother had not yet started school in England. I can remember the Kavirondo or crown-crested cranes that stalked about the garden and being stung by a bee. After six months' leave in England, we spent about six months in Nairobi and Jean was born there.

My first real memories are of our next posting and life in Thika – a ghastly treeless place. It was at Thika that the Blue Post Hotel (shown in the film *Out of Africa*) was the socialising venue for Colony officials and also settlers and coffee planters. My mother, left on her own night after night while my father went to play bridge, became quite unhappy.

Here my mother gave me my first lessons – sums on a slate, copy book writing and reading, 'The cat is on the mat' sort of thing, and even a bit of French – 'La plume de ma tante.' Apparently I would speak Swahili like a native. My mother, speaking to me in

English, would tell me to go to the house-boy or ayah and give one of them a message. Speaking to them in Swahili, I would return to my mother and speak to her in Swahili!

Bush animals were a large part of my life. I was given two young 'dik-diks' (young deer) as pets. Once on a walk to the nearby river where we had our vegetable gardens we saw, as so often happened, the havoc created by the hippos which would come up out of the river and trample all over the maize and other vegetables. On another occasion when we were there one evening, coming up the river we saw two round objects shining like electric light bulbs; the rest of the hippo was completely submerged.

Our next tour was to the Baringo–Rift Valley District at a hill station called Kabarnet – a rather lovely station – high up and cool. It was quite beautiful with very tall shady trees in the garden. At first I had a governess and through my parents she met and soon after married a PWD road engineer. Due to this I was then sent as a boarder to the Loretto Convent, a Girls' Roman Catholic School near Nairobi.

In Kabarnet at first we lived in a wood and corrugated-iron house until a brand-new house was built for the District Commissioner, and this is where my younger sister Susan was born. I was away at school at the time and can remember feeling very cheated when the nuns told me the news that I had a new baby sister, having opened the letter which my mother sent me.

It was while living in this house that an unpleasant happening occurred. The African cook got drunk on their very potent banana beer and assaulted the ayah who came screaming to our house from the servants' quarters. The outcome was that he was clapped into jail for a cooling-off period.

Another frightening experience, when we were living in Thika, was a bad earth tremor late one night. At the time we had guests who were sleeping in a tent in the garden. Suddenly everything started to jump up and down where it was standing, so we ran from the house and joined our friends in their tent for some time until we felt all danger had passed. It was a most unpleasant experience.

In the early pioneering days in Kenya it was an unwritten law that you never went out in the sun without wearing your pith helmet, otherwise, they said, the sun would drive you mad. I remember hating those helmets because they were very hard and uncomfortable and restricted one's play. It wasn't until about the 1930s that the belief about your head being exposed to too much sun was discounted and the wearing of helmets began to be relaxed.

When I was at the Loretto Convent, I was quite unhappy. I was frightened of the nuns who were great disciplinarians and were really very harsh towards the pupils. Maybe it was because I wasn't an RC that I bore the brunt so much, but I always seemed to be getting into trouble or getting the blame.

The school was an open-plan building and was really very vulnerable. Once a mad African came very near the school when the RC church and the convent were celebrating Corpus Christi. We ran in to report it and he was soon led away. The pupils were responsible for laying out beautiful patterns and designs in cut flower heads on the tree-lined road from the school up to the church and later this was all walked over by the procession of followers. Not being a Catholic, I did not know what the significance the pathway of flowers had but I can remember thinking what a horrible waste of beautiful flowers it was.

The food at the convent was not particularly memorable except a rather good banana fool which we were given only as a great treat and on which we gorged, going up for four or five helpings.

I was taught piano by a very stern Mother Mary who put the fear of death in me by rapping my knuckles if I could not play the piece or scales I had been told to practise. And when I failed my first piano exam because I hadn't a piano at Kabarnet to practise on in the holidays, I felt as though I was condemned to Eternal Fire.

I don't remember my violin lessons at the convent, but I remember those my mother gave me on a dear little half-sized violin. Those lessons were fun, but at the convent I was put at the back of the 2nd violins in the orchestra to sink or swim and mostly I sank. I can only remember playing a note here or there (mostly there) and not enjoying taking part at all. And it did nothing for my nerves later in my life when I had to perform.

Two incidents which I can recall affected me considerably in my tender years. My parents used to listen to a crystal radio set and one evening it was announced that the R101 airship had exploded and gone up in flames and everyone on board had lost their lives. Another evening while listening to the radio, suddenly two Askaris (Kenyan police – their uniform was khaki drill shirt and shorts and legs covered with navy puttees) burst into the sitting room and clapped handcuffs on my father's wrists. His drink went flying out of his hand and I became almost hysterical seeing my father treated like this. Then suddenly the whole mood changed to laughter when the real identity of the two Askaris was realised. They were a couple of young Englishmen who were visiting the area and had done this for a huge prank, blackening their faces, arms and legs most realistically. After a time, they managed to console me, and everyone had a great laugh about it all.

From Kabarnet we came home to England. My mother, my two sisters and I never returned to Kenya because of our education. My father returned as he was an established district officer in the Crown Agent's Service. We lived in my Grandfather Rimington's old Georgian family house in Penrith which had been left to my father. Tynefield, as it was called, was quite a lovely old house, but oh, so cold. The grounds were extensive – kitchen garden, fruit garden and lawns which meant a lot of work to keep up. It was ideal for a young growing family, especially as there was a tennis court, a large wooden practice board and a tumbledown, old, castle-style livery man's quarters in which we played even although it was terribly dangerous as the floor boards were rotting away.

Tynefield was a spacious old Georgian house with a large drawing-room and a room called the Library in the front of the house, both looking out onto the front lawn which was also the tennis court. Behind these two rooms was a large dining-room, a large kitchen and plenty of sundry offices and cellars downstairs. The best feature of the house was its central staircase with mahogany handrail. This was featured in a television advertisement some years ago when it was seen with a dog running down the stairs. Outside the back door was a courtyard leading to all the domestic work areas such as washroom and coalhouse. The house is now a grade II listed building and is used as a funeral business.

One cannot forget the faithful maidservant my grandparents employed who had been with them so long that she seemed to be part of the house. She was called Emma Powell, who I feel most strongly had been imported from the West Indies as cheap labour. She had frizzy black hair and spoke with the accent peculiar to the islanders of mixed parentage who lived in those parts. She was good at her job and ran the house efficiently. She served my grandparents for many years, and then went on to Aunt Evie. Eventually she retired and was able to buy herself a little car and enjoy her retirement. My mother nicknamed her 'Lady Powell'. The other old timer was 'Old May' the gardener, and there is the lovely story of him coming into the kitchen one day and announcing to Emma, 'H'Emma, them h'onions h'is ready to coom h'oop.'

Jean and I went for lessons to a retired primary school teacher called Mrs Purdy who lived in Lowther Street. She was quite forbidding in appearance, but was a very good teacher and gave us a thorough basic education in the three R's. We weren't frightened of her, and she was very kind to us, inviting us to tea once a year.

I continued my piano lessons with a Miss Westmoreland who lived only a stone's throw from Mrs Purdy. She was a good teacher also, especially in Theory of Music. She kept putting me in for exams which I hated; even so, I seemed to do quite well in them.

I remember my first school at the bottom of Wordsworth Street and how terrified I was of everything. Even to where I had to hang my coat and hat though my nameplate was clearly above the peg. I remember doing sums in a book with squared paper which was far superior to doing them on a slate. Also having to write short stories – mine were very short. Art was great fun and I brought home paper windmills and doll's house furniture made from chestnuts, pins and wool.

The school uniform consisted of a navy-blue serge pleated tunic worn over a long-sleeved white blouse; I absolutely hated the hat which was like a box. I particularly hated 'Liberty' bodices which we had to wear over a vest to keep our kidneys warm. Also they were a means by which, when we began to wear stockings, we could fix clip-on suspenders. I also hated button-up knickers because the buttonholes were forever becoming larger; consequently the buttons slipped out and you can guess what happened then. They were also at the side so quite difficult to do up or undo in a hurry. I was very glad when elasticated knickers came into fashion. I always wanted a pair of shiny black patent leather shoes with ankle strap fastenings, but my mother would not allow me to have them, saying they were very common. Quite probably they were but a lot of my friends at school wore them, so what do you deduce from that?

Fortunately we were never fed on bread and dripping though I was horrified when we were invited for tea in the nursery with the children of a doctor's family and the Nanny produced bread and dripping. They gobbled it up, but I just could not bring myself to eat it and I remember that great scorn poured on me.

My favourite sweeties were Ogo-pogo eyes/Gob-stoppers (aniseed balls) which we could buy at two for a halfpenny. They had a strange flavour but they lasted a long time, which made them even more of a bargain. There were also liquorice wheels and sherbet bags, which one sucked up through a liquorice tube, and if you weren't careful the sherbet went up your nose.

A good buy was a penny packet of Smith's crisps containing a little twisted blue bag of salt – usually found right at the bottom of the bag so you couldn't get at it until you had almost finished the crisps.

When Grandfather Thomas came to stay he would take Jean and me off to Dayson's Dairy – a real dairy with stone-flag floors and shining churns of milk and cream and an all-pervading smell of milk fat and cream. He would buy us a penny ice cream cornet or sandwich (slider) which contained pure dairy ice cream, and we would enjoy licking them all the way back to Tynefield. Mother would regularly send Jean and me to buy fresh yeast from a little old yeast shop in Angel Lane. We liked doing this because the little old lady who kept the shop had a box of jelly babies on the counter and she would give us one each, always asking us which colour we wanted; I always asked for a black one.

Soon I was old enough for secondary school and was sent to Carlisle High School, where I became a weekly boarder, travelling by train from Penrith to Carlisle on Monday and returning home for the weekend on a Friday.

A year or so later Jean joined me and we continued there until we came to the end of our schooldays. For the most part I was very happy at the High School, enjoying the sports in particular.

We had a lot of odd teachers – the two Misses Wynnes; Miss P. Wynne was very tall and with head held high strode into the classroom with a bundle of tomes under her arm. Miss M. Wynne, her sister, was head of the Junior department and was more subdued in manner. Then there was Miss Smyth whom we said must have been crossed in love because she always broke down and wept when reciting 'The Charge of the Light Brigade' to us. Miss Batty, the Art mistress, was as thin as a rake and spoke in very mincing tones. Miss Heath 'taught' history by dictating endless notes at every lesson followed by an expected ten-page essay for homework.

My music flourished under Miss Carey and for one year under Miss Holgate who took over while Miss Carey went off around the world to broaden her horizons. Miss Carey was an excellent piano teacher, having trained at the Royal College of Music, and she was very keen to see me go on to train there. I finished at school with a Distinction in Grade VII, and at the same time the examiner also advised me to have training in Music, which I did even though World War Two had broken out and all my class mates were joining up in the Women's Forces for the glamour or else. I suffered days and days of indecision and misery trying to decide which way to go and finally decided to train as a teacher of Music.

Appendix 1

Hypolite Joseph Emil Germain Cornillon; silhouette by August Edouart, Edinburgh, 17 February 1830

The following is taken from a newspaper cutting dated 1913 pasted on the back of the silhouette's frame.

Edouart, who was born in 1789, practised his art chiefly in the United Kingdom and in America. He was in Edinburgh in 1831, when the exiled king of France, Charles X, and a small suite, resided at Holyrood, and during that time he seems to have made many portraits in black silhouette, not only of the French king and his courtiers, but also of the leading citizens and of the 'landed gentry and aristocracy' in the neighbourhood, whose houses he visited, and of the humbler people who visited his studio.

He left behind him a large and remarkable series of such silhouette portraits, which came to light not long since in a curious manner. M. Edouart, it appears, kept a duplicate of every portrait he did, and pasted it into a portfolio. He also named and dated them. These records of his art he carried about with him. He went to America in 1839 and resided in New York, practising his art there for ten years. On his return to Europe in 1849 the ship in which he sailed, the *Oneida*, was wrecked off the coast of Guernsey. No lives were lost, and part of the baggage, including apparently M. Edouart's precious portfolio, was saved. The artist was hospitably received by a family of the name of Lukis, residing on the island. Sometime ago a lady, Mrs F. Nevill Jackson, who was writing on silhouettes, put a small notice in the *Connoisseur* magazine asking if the owners of silhouette collections would allow her to examine any interesting examples, and among the answers came the offer of the folio volumes which the writer recognised as the long-lost reference folios of August Edouart. It was found that the owner was the son of Frederica Lukis, of Guernsey, to whom the artist had given his collection on his recovery from illness and shock after the shipwreck.

An alphabetical list of the portraits, over 5,000 in number, has now been compiled. They measure about seven or eight inches; all are full length except about fifty, which are of the bust only, and with the exception of about fifty were all taken from life. They are often of great value to the descendants on account of the rarity of other pictorial records, as well as the perfect accuracy of the likeness.

The report concluded with a list of the silhouette portraits acquired in 1913 for the Scottish National Portrait Gallery where they can still be seen.

Appendix 2

Commemoration of the Death
of
Frances Emily Hill Rimington

F RANCES Emily Hill Rimington died in Yorkshire on
27th December, 1973.

In her memory two trees have been planted:

Prunus subhirtella autumnalis (*rosea*) in the Bellie
Churchyard, Fochabers, Morayshire, where the 4th
duke of Gordon and his second wife, Jean Christie, her
great-great grandparents, are buried. This tree was a
favourite of hers and flowers in winter around the time
of her birthday, December 20th.

Camellia 'Donation', a double pink variety, at the
National Trust property of Brodie Castle, near Forres.

The 5th duke of Gordon married Elizabeth Brodie,
who was responsible for many good works in the area.

Appendix 3

From the Obituary of Mr John Thomas

DEATH OF MR JOHN THOMAS
FORMERLY SHERIFF CLERK OF PERTHSHIRE
NOTABLE CAREER

Mr John Thomas, who only so recently as 30th June resigned his appointment as Sheriff Clerk of Perthshire, passed away at his residence, 25 Barossa Place, Perth, late on Friday night. Mr Thomas had been in failing health for the past six months, but his indomitable spirit and clear head saw him at his official duties in the County Buildings and at church on Sundays till almost the last. Due to an inward trouble Mr Thomas underwent an operation in Edinburgh three years ago, and despite his great age he came well through it. He seemed his old energetic and genial self again for a time, but age began to tell on him. When he felt the labour of walking from his residence to the Courtroom he drove in a cab and returned by the same means. He devoted his evenings to letter-writing and reading or conversation with a friend who might drop in, and was as fresh as ever for business next morning.

Mr Thomas has passed away in his 88th year, having been born in November 1826. For years past his recurring birthdays have been the greatest source of pleasure to himself and to others – for others to send and for him to receive congratulations. One of the most appreciated was that of two years ago when he had sent to him a floral cricket bat, the blade of which was labelled – '86, not out.'

Mr Thomas came of an old Perth family who were in the vintner trade. His father became a solicitor in Perth, and the late Mr Thomas followed in his footsteps. Much of his success was his own. He was a good man of business. He seemed ever able to see the end from the beginning, and without causing friction or appearing to rush matters was able to take the shortest cut to the end in view.

As fully reported in our columns at the time of Mr Thomas' retiral from the Sheriff Clerkship, he had a long law career. He was educated at Kinoull School and Perth Academy, was in Edinburgh for a time passing his law examinations, and returned to Perth and entered his father's office. Later, he entered into partnership and the firm of Messrs Thomas and MacLeish, solicitors, was and is one of the best known and successful in Perth.

For a short time Mr Thomas was a town councillor, and later Police Commission and Town Clerk. In 1874 he was appointed Sheriff Clerk for Perthshire and Commissary Clerk. He was also Clerk of the Guildry Incorporation, a position he greatly appreciated, and brought out a small volume on the history of the Perth Guildry.

He was Liberal agent for Perth County and Perth City for years, and was the life-long friend of the late Mr C.S. Parker, M.P. for Perth County and afterwards for Perth City. He was also agent for the Hon. Arthur Kinnaird.

His honorary offices were many. He was never weary in doing something for the good of others, and for years was a Director and Secretary of Perth County and City Infirmary, the same for the Fechney Industrial School, for the Perth Poor and Sick Societies, Old Men's Indigent Society, and member of the Perthshire Society of Solicitors and the Edinburgh Perthshire Society, and many others. Mr Thomas was as ready to help with his purse as with his hand and head.

Mr Thomas was also a keen Churchman, and for over 50 years an elder and member of St Paul's Parish Church. His labour for St Paul's and his many subscriptions to it were ever a labour of love and pleasure. Two years ago he collaborated with Mr Peter Baxter in the issuing of a history of St Paul's Church, and at his own expense sent many copies to former members of the congregation in Colonial and other parts and also presented a copy to every family in St Paul's.

Glossary

Angels on horseback	Oysters and bacon on toast.
Aniline	Product of coal tar used in dying and other processes.
Arrowroot	Nutritious starch from the rhizome of the West Indian plant of the same name.
Askari	East Africa soldier or policeman.
Barracoat	Flannel coat worn by an infant; a wrapper for a baby; woman's undergarment.
Bassinet pram	Deeply welled pram.
Black leading	Application of the mineral plumbago to preserve a black finish on a kitchen range.
Brougham	One-horse, closed carriage.
Brush braid	Strong fabric woven in a narrow band.
Chiffonier	Ornamental cabinet.
Chintz	Cotton printed generally in several colours on a white or light background.

Chrystoleum	*see* Oleograph.
Combinations	Under-garment comprising vest and drawers.
Corsage	Bodice or waist of a woman's dress.
Crêpe de chine	Thin fabric made from silk.
Devilled bones	Bones cooked by grilling with mustard.
Dik-dik	Very small antelope found in East Africa, species of Madoqua.
Drugget	Woven and felted coarse woollen fabric.
Fichu-lace	Three cornered cape with two ends crossed upon the bosom.
Fish-tail gas jet	Early gas light with a double jet, small flame.
Flux	Discharge from the mucous membrane.
Frieze	Rough, heavy woollen cloth.
Gimp	Trimming, e.g. on soft furnishings.
Governess cart	Light low two-wheeled vehicle with face-to-face seats at the side.
Grosgrain	Heavy corded silk.
Growler	Four-wheeled, horse-drawn cab.
Hairst Monday	The Monday occurring about four weeks before the anticipated start of the harvest, the day when harvest labour was hired.
Half-tester	Canopy over part (but not all) of the bed.

Incandescent gas burners	Lighting where gas heats the mantle in order to emit a white light.
Inverness cape	Long coat or ulster with a wide, sometimes removable, cape.
Japanned	Varnished or lacquered in glossy black.
Knot bugles	Hat trimming of beads tied in loops and clumps.
Landau	(Horse drawn) carriage with folding top.
Lawn	Fine linen.
Leg o'mutton sleeve	Sleeve tight at the wrist and full above.
Liberty bodice	A warm undergarment worn by females, on top of a woollen vest, with suspenders attached front and back.
Memsahib	In India, a married European lady.
Moire	Watered mohair, silk or other material with watered appearance.
Ninon	Thin semi-transparent material.
Oleograph	A kind of chromo lithograph made to look like an art painting.
Pifferari men	Itinerant musicians who played more than one instrument simultaneously – from 'piffero', a fife, Italian bagpipe or a crude oboe.
Pilch	Flannel cloth for wrapping a child.
Piqué	Stiff corded cotton fabric.

Plush	Fabric with a longer and more open pile than velvet.
Rusty	Rustic in the sense of rough and crudely made.
Sairey Gamp	An untidy lady, a character in Charles Dickens's *Martin Chuzzlewit*.
Saperlipopette	Mild French oath.
Sarsenet	Thin tissue of fine silk.
Shantung	Plain, rough cloth of wild silk.
Slit trench	Narrow trench for one or more people.
Slouch hat	Soft, broad-brimmed hat.
Spencer	Woman's short jacket-style undergarment.
Stangen	Crisp bread fingers. From German *Stange*, a bun.
Swans' down, swansdown	Under-plumage of a swan, fine woollen or mixed material.
Wagonette	Open carriage with two seats crosswise in front and two back seats arranged lengthways and facing inwards.
Whole hunter watch	Pocket watch with metal cover protecting the entire face.